CHEF'S**GARDEN**

TERENCE CONRAN

CHEF'S**GARDEN**

WITH ANDI CLEVELY

RECIPES BY JEREMY LEE

SPECIAL PHOTOGRAPHY BY GEORGIA GLYNN-SMITH
AND NICOLA BROWNE

conran
OCTOPUS

contents

For Jonathan and Ian
Barton Court's green fingers

First published in 1999 by
Conran Octopus Limited
a part of Octopus Publishing Group
2–4 Heron Quays
London E14 4JP

Text, design and layout copyright
© Conran Octopus 1999
Recipe copyright © Jeremy Lee 1999
Special photography copyright
© Georgia Glynn-Smith 1999
© Nicola Browne 1999

Commissioning Editor: Stuart Cooper
Project Editor: Paula Hardy
Editor: Carole McGlynn
Editorial Assistant: Maxine McCaghy
Art Editor and Design: Vanessa Courtier
Project Consultant: Simon Willis
Picture Research: Jess Walton
Special Photography:
Georgia Glynn-Smith, Nicola Browne
Recipes: Jeremy Lee
Food stylist: Maxine Clarke
Stylists: Róisín Neild, Gilly Love,
Penny Markham
Production Controller: Zoë Fawcett

British Library Cataloguing-in-Publication Data
A catalogue record for this book is
available from the British Library

ISBN 1 84091 070 4

Printed in Italy

Growing vegetables has always been one of my passions. As a small boy, I would work away in my parents' vegetable plot, primarily because we needed to grow and tend vegetables to feed the family but also because I was fascinated by the whole growing process, from the emergence of the first seedlings to the subsequent 'Jack and the Beanstalk' growth. But it was not until my first visits to France and Italy that I really developed a love of fruit and vegetables. I saw in the markets the very sights that had opened the eyes of Elizabeth David. In *Italian Food* she describes a Venetian market where: 'the cabbages are cobalt blue, the beetroots deep rose, the lettuces pure clear green, sharp as glass. Bunches of gaudy marrow flowers show off the elegance of pink and white marbled bean pods, primrose potatoes, green plums, green peas.' Not only did the experience awaken my aesthetic sensibilities, it also kindled my passion for real food, firmly connected to the soil.

There are few activities in life more pleasurable than going to a market in France, Italy or Spain and choosing a basketful of the freshest vegetables, fruit, fish and cheese. Just as exciting is the experience of spreading the produce out on the kitchen table and being inspired to cook a simple but wonderful meal. The only thing that surpasses this sense of satisfaction is to have grown the vegetables and fruit yourself, sowing seeds, nurturing the young plants, watching them grow and finally harvesting them at the peak of perfection. Not only will you take pride in what you have achieved in your garden but, more importantly, the taste of your produce will be fuller and more intense. Many vegetables and fruit have a fugitive flavour which they lose rapidly once they are picked. A friend's father was so passionate about asparagus that he placed a large pan of water on a Primus stove at the end of the asparagus row and ran down the row, cutting the spears and throwing them into the boiling water. Perhaps this is going a bit far, but if you are really interested in the flavour of food, growing it yourself and cooking it within minutes of harvest will increase your enjoyment and reward your taste buds.

My love of good food inspired this book and the Chef's Roof Garden at the 1999 Chelsea Flower Show (featured as a case study on pages 36–9). I hope that anybody who shares this passion will consider establishing a kitchen garden because, as the book shows, you really can grow vegetables, fruit and herbs in small spaces and containers. Growing your own not only brings pleasure but allows you to experiment with varieties that are unavailable in your local shop or supermarket. These can make a significant difference to your enjoyment of food and could give you, as the Italians say, *saltimbocca* (a leap in the mouth). The bonus is that the vegetable garden can be a place of beauty in itself – competition, to my mind, to any herbaceous border, and an ideal way of satisfying all the senses at once.

introduction

TERENCE CONRAN'S GARDEN AT BARTON COURT

CONTEMPORARY SIMPLICITY IN THE URBAN CHEF'S GARDEN

design

Once you have decided to invest in flavour and grow your own fruit, vegetables or herbs, it is tempting to start sowing and planting immediately. Experience shows, however, that a little preliminary attention to planning and design is the surest way to translate your dreams into reality, especially if your garden is small and your ambition boundless.

Every gardener eventually has to accept that there is never enough room to grow everything, but with good design even the tiniest plot can be a corner of paradise. You will need to abandon preconceived notions of long, widely spaced rows, manure by the cartload or double-digging according to ancient rotation rules. The traditional methods associated with grand kitchen gardens simply do not apply to the modern backyard, patio, roof garden or balcony.

Instead, there are ways of turning limitations to advantage and maximizing yields by making full use of every corner and niche. Edible crops can be mingled with flowers to make an exuberant and truly mixed border, or tucked into window-boxes with summer annuals. Or you might prefer a formal potager of patterned beds, or simply a collection of pots to provide a summer supply of salads.

TRADITIONAL ROWS OF CROPS

Transferring a plan from drawing board
to the ground is easy if you can first
clear the site and cultivate the soil
thoroughly (opposite). Here, simple
symmetrical beds have been marked
out and edged with treated boards to
define the growing areas, intersected
by ample paths of levelled gravel.
The comparatively severe geometry of
the design is soon softened as young
herbs and vegetables begin to grow
lustily in the fresh, fertile soil.

FIRST STEPS

There is no stereotypical garden and, similarly, every gardener is unique. In
planning a kitchen garden you should start with yourself – with your aims and
culinary tastes, but also with your capabilities. Plant a shrub, and it may thrive
even if you rarely water or prune it, whereas food crops need commitment if
they are to achieve the abundance and quality latent in every packet of seeds.

Examine honestly all those factors which will inevitably influence the final
plan. Decide how much time you can devote to the garden, especially at the
busiest seasons: spring, when so much needs sowing and planting out, and
autumn, when many crops are cleared or gathered in for storing. If you have a
plot of open ground, it will need digging, at least initially, and this may make
unfamiliar demands on stamina and energy. Plants in pots have to be watered
regularly, often daily in hot weather, and batches of seedlings will not wait
indefinitely to be planted out. One way to halve the amount of time and work
required is to buy your crops as strips of small plants from the garden centre,
rather than raising them from seed yourself. This is particularly appropriate in
small town gardens where space is also limited. The demands of a kitchen
garden are not excessive, but it is easy to overlook them while fired with the
urge to get started.

Assessing the site   Take a good look at the space available for your crops.
The ideal is an empty prepared site, such as you might have in a brand new
garden. It may be levelled and ready for you to superimpose a plan, or to make
a terrace ready for container planting. Or you could have a patch of grassland
or a recently vacated building site with imported topsoil thinly spread over
bricks and builder's rubble – deal with this first, and you will then have a clear

site and plenty of design options (see Garden Styles, page 14). In reality, the garden is more likely to be partly or fully established, and you may prefer to start by experimenting with a few herbs and vegetables tucked in among existing plants, expanding the range of crops and dedicating more room to them as increasing confidence and space permit. Some food plants could be substituted for ornamentals: a grapevine where you might grow a wisteria, for example, rosemary or raspberries instead of a leafy hedge, redcurrant fans rather than cotoneaster on a fence, or a trained gooseberry as a centrepiece to a bed in place of a standard rose.

BREAKING WITH TRADITION
Traditional kitchen gardens (right)
emphasize order and discipline, with
plants marshalled in long, parallel rows
to allow easy access for cultivation and
harvest. In a small garden this can be
an extravagant use of space and may
present a rather utilitarian landscape,
so you need to find more imaginative
ways of incorporating food plants.

Other growing spaces Where there is no open ground, explore areas that
might support a few food crops. Hard surfaces such as a patio or courtyard, a
terrace, alley or balcony can be furnished with pots and other containers, some
permanent, others changed seasonally as crops develop. Climbing and trailing
crops such as runner beans or a grapevine, planted in the ground or in
containers, can be trained over fences and walls or grown on a pergola or
metal archway to create a tunnel over an alleyway, extending the cultivated

area and adding a vertical dimension to your design. Provided it is easily accessible, a rooftop can be transformed into a flourishing garden, while a small, steady harvest of vegetables, herbs and even fruits like strawberries can be gathered from a window box. Windowsills (indoors and out), ledges, tops of low walls and even the sides of steps can all be used as growing spaces.

If lack of space is a real problem, it might be best to concentrate on small indispensable plants such as herbs and salads which need to be fresh and close at hand, and explore the option of renting an allotment or some spare land nearby for larger, more demanding crops. An allotment provides a substantial extension to the garden in a social context, with other keen kitchen gardeners to support and encourage you with advice, assistance and often an exchange of seeds or plants.

Planning the crops   Having sized up the available space, you can decide what to grow. There is unlikely to be room for every crop you would like, or for large quantities of the chosen few. Trimming your plans to match the site might be disheartening at first, but the tiniest patch will usually support more produce than at first seems possible.

If you are not used to working with space, draw a ground plan on a sheet of paper: a simple, roughly measured sketch will help you to clarify and organize your thoughts. Indicate the position of the house and the garden's main structures, such as paths, fences, walls, and sheds; note, too, where the sun rises and sets. Mark out existing flower beds and any trees, and identify where shade is cast by overhanging branches from neighbouring trees as well as from buildings. Armed with this information, you can begin to allocate suitable growing areas and sites for larger plants, and plant them out so as to make maximum use of the available space.

CHOOSING WHAT TO GROW

Identify those crops you regard as indispensable – special favourites, including any you use frequently in the kitchen, as well as vegetables, fruit and herbs that are not sold in supermarkets or that have a fugitive flavour. Salads and herbs, for example, are a universal and easily grown ingredient. List your most desirable crops and familiarize yourself with their needs in terms of space, aspect and time required to reach maturity, then work out where to grow them. If you have limited space, decide whether quantity is important or diversity, as is the case below, where small, brick-enclosed beds are packed with a lavish selection of herbs.

GARDEN STYLES

At this stage, it is a good idea to consider the style of garden with which you feel most comfortable. Browse for ideas in as many good gardening books and magazines as you can find, including some of those published in France, the home of the potager where kitchen gardening has been refined into an art form. Pruning fruit trees and bushes to fit into restricted spaces is an old French skill, due for revival to meet the constraints imposed by today's small plots. Restored medieval gardens can be an inspiration too: many are organized around small beds of herbs, flowers and vegetables grown together, as was the custom when use and beauty often co-existed.

The Château de Villandry, just west of Tours, is perhaps the most famous and lavishly planted French ornamental potager and a potent source of ideas, with its use of contrasting colours in the vegetable beds, while the Italian botanical garden at Padua is a classic example of elegant design with small formal beds, both square and circular in shape. At the other end of the scale, the humble allotment, where gardeners have experimented with all kinds of design to make the most of a limited plot, can be a source of inspiration. Allow your imagination to play with balanced arrangements of beds and paths that make the garden an inviting place to be. It should be interesting to look at and a joy to work in. Keep your plan bold and simple, with a few wide paths and large beds – these can be subdivided with fruit fences, stepping stones or paths of trodden earth. Avoid intricate designs: a maze of tiny patches can look fussy and is all too soon filled with plants.

Within these outlines you can disperse crops according to your preferred style. If you find the orderliness of kitchen garden rows intensely satisfying, use a garden line (a length of string stretched taut between two wooden pegs) to

GOOD-LOOKING CROPS
Even in the dedicated kitchen garden, edible plants often have great impact. The contrasting leaf shapes of flowering beetroot, sweet corn and squashes add drama to neatly hedged beds (above), while cabbage and carrot foliage enhances the colour and form of a rose hedge (opposite).

ensure straight edges, measure distances accurately, and plant in square, rectangular or triangular blocks. Allocate a special bed for fruit and other perennials, or confine these to corners and edges. For a more decorative plot, consider creating a formal potager within a pattern of beds (see pages 20–3). If this is too formal, or too much effort, simply blend handsome crops among the flowers in your borders (see opposite page).

MEETING PLANTS' NEEDS

However pleasing your design on paper, it is no use if little sun penetrates the site you have chosen. It is vital to consider not only aspect but all the other practical, everyday needs of crops if your kitchen garden is to succeed. So identify the conditions likely to affect productive growth, and you will appreciate both the problems and opportunities involved in creating a kitchen garden.

Light Most crops need plenty of sunlight to keep them sturdy, vigorous and growing actively. Hot direct sun in summer may cause heat stress when the roots cannot take up water fast enough, and providing light shade during this season can prevent leafy crops such as lettuce or spinach from racing to seed, but otherwise maximum light is the ideal. Make sure overhanging tree branches and tall hedges do not block light – it is often possible to thin tree canopies and prune hedges to improve light penetration without compromising their role as shelter. Many town gardens are subject to shade cast by high walls. Painting the walls white will increase the amount of light reflected onto plants, as will using pale paving and mulching materials.

Warmth Soil and air temperatures need to be several degrees above freezing to support growth. Walk round the garden on a cold day and note where sunlight falls early in the morning or where frost lingers longest, to identify the warmest and coolest spots. Reserve the least frost-prone parts of the garden for early sowings, cold frames, tender perennials and plants like rhubarb for forcing. Keep the hottest, sunniest positions for Mediterranean herbs and tender summer crops such as tomatoes, peppers and sweet corn. Laying straw, cloches or pieces of glass or polythene over the ground for two weeks before sowing will raise soil temperatures significantly in early spring; in very cold gardens, concentrate on relatively hardy vegetables and salads, such as carrots, cos lettuce and parsley, as well as perennial herbs and late-flowering or early-ripening fruit varieties.

Moisture Moist soil or compost is essential for sustained growth: without it, seeds will not germinate and plant roots cannot absorb any nutrients. Supplementary watering with a can or a hose may eventually become essential, especially for plants grown in containers, but the time when you need to start this can be delayed by raising the level of humus in the soil. Humus is created partially by decayed organic material, usually supplied by additions of garden compost, leafmould, well-rotted manure or recycled potting compost, which all hold moisture and prevent early drying out. Add as much organic

CHERISHING YOUR PLANTS
Most vegetables and other food crops are not native to our gardens, and they need tending to make sure they give of their best. A little regular attention to ensure that they are well watered and fed is enough to prevent any seasonal stresses which could reduce yields. Check their welfare daily in summer, especially moisture-loving crops that are ripening such as the tomatoes and aubergines shown opposite, or container-grown plants such as the kumquat and herbs pictured below.

Exposure to frost and cold winds can be mitigated by sheltering susceptible crops. An existing wall, fence or hedge will divert or filter the wind and shield plants for a distance up to ten times its height. Wind protection is particularly important for early-flowering and late-ripening fruits, best trained on a warm, sheltered wall. Reinforce this beneficial influence within the garden by creating low divisions of rosemary or lavender hedges, training rows of raspberries, currants or gooseberries as cordons or fans on wires, or making temporary windbreaks of tall crops like sweet corn or Jerusalem artichokes. Plants growing on open balconies and roof gardens can be shielded up to a certain height by a parapet wall (opposite), which can be extended if necessary by erecting panels of split bamboo or filter screens of trained ivy and similar evergreen climbers.

matter as possible when first preparing beds, then lightly turn more into the surface whenever you sow or plant another crop. Dress permanent plants such as fruit annually with a layer of compost or decayed manure. Most herbs thrive with little humus, however, and too much can be harmful. Mulching keeps soils moist, and many materials can be used for this: in addition to those mentioned, try grass clippings, partly decayed leaves, straw, shredded bark, and wet newspapers or polythene disguised with a thin layer of soil on top. Spent mushroom compost also makes a good mulch but contains lime: if used in large amounts it can change the acidity of the soil. Grass clippings used regularly in any quantity can increase the soil's acidity: use around raspberries, which like acid conditions, or over mushroom compost to balance its alkalinity.

Fertility Plants need a balanced range of nutrients to ensure healthy growth, in the same way as we do. Adding garden compost or decayed manure annually will supply variable, generally small amounts of fertility, which can be supplemented with proprietary fertilizers, especially when growth is active: in early spring, for example, or when plants are flowering or fruiting, a feed can be a welcome tonic. The limited supply of fertilizers in potting composts is usually exhausted about six weeks after planting, and regular feeding every one to two weeks then becomes essential.

Use a general or balanced fertilizer, containing all the necessary nutrients, or a high-potash feed for colour and flavour (rose and tomato feeds, for example). Feeds high in nitrogen foster leaf growth at the expense of fruits: apply them to stimulate young plants into making fast growth. Always use liquid feeds for container-grown plants; powdered or granular fertilizers are suitable for plants grown in open ground, and should be applied when the soil is moist. (For a summary of routine plant care, see pages 136–9.)

CROPPING PLANS

A good cropping plan maximizes a bed's potential. Never leave the ground bare: as one crop is cleared, transplant another into the space after adding compost to the soil. This may mean starting the follow-on crop elsewhere, in a nursery bed or in trays, so it is ready to take over immediately. Alternatively, sow direct, as shown above, where the seedlings of successional rows of carrots and lettuces have emerged and are ready for thinning. In the background the next plot has been prepared for further sowings.

PLOTS AND POTAGERS

A traditional kitchen garden is usually sown and planted with long rows spaced widely apart so that you can walk comfortably between them. But you might prefer to divide your plot into a series of beds, small enough to be dug over and planted in an hour or two and easily manageable from an adjacent path without treading on the soil. Grouping crops in specially cultivated beds allows you to concentrate fertility where it is needed and makes economical use of a small space. There are two kinds of productive bed: raised beds, built to lift the working level to a more comfortable height, and deep beds – small areas of ground intensively cultivated for prolific long-term cropping.

Raised beds   Enclosed by retaining walls, raised beds can vary widely in height, depending on their purpose, and offer flexible design potential. Sides 45cm (18in) high allow a sufficient depth of soil to grow most crops, and can solve the problem of making a garden on a hard surface or on badly drained soil. Lower sides – 30cm (12in) – can transform a sloping site into a series of terraced beds, but should be built on a soil base for increased growing depth lest their shallow contents dry out in summer. Waist-high beds, 75–90cm (30–36in) above ground, elevate the working height for less agile gardeners. The walls may be made from brick, stone or treated timber; leave holes in the base or gaps low down in the sides for efficient drainage on hard surfaces.

Deep beds   If you decide on a deep bed, preparing it will be hard work, but the initial labour should not need repeating for a long time. Mark out the bed, making it as long as you like but no more than 90cm–1.2m (3–4ft) wide so that all parts can be tended without treading on the soil. Double-dig the ground (that is, down to two spades' depth) and work in plenty of rotted manure, mushroom compost or another bagged source of organic material throughout the bed's full depth. Finish with a mulch of this organic material; lightly fork in more whenever you sow or plant, and mulch the bed again every autumn. This will keep the soil fertile for up to ten years.

Deep beds need some kind of edging and the character of the surrounding garden will influence your choice. Plants form the simplest edging to paths: use neat, mat-forming perennials, from pinks and thrift to thymes and other prostrate herbs. Timber gravel boards, railway sleepers or wooden poles laid on their sides suit deep beds with straight edges; create a more ornamental effect by nailing roofing tiles to the outside. Pliable stems of willow, hazel or laburnum, woven like shallow basketwork between short pegs, suit rural

The formal symmetry of the potager is designed for both aesthetic appeal and practical usefulness. There are many different layouts but they are all based on the geometry of the square, the circle or the triangle, or a combination of these shapes. Paths are a powerful element of the design and help to define the pattern of beds, as well as providing access for care and harvest. They can be made from weathered bricks, setts, textured paving slabs, bark or gravel. Main paths should be about 45–60cm (18–24in) wide, while any paths meant to accommodate a wheelbarrow need to be at least 90cm (3ft) wide.

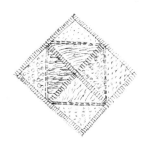

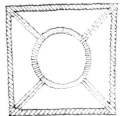

locations and can be used for beds with straight or curved edges. Edgings of brick and stone (mortared or laid dry) are ideal for shaped or raised beds; paint them with yogurt to encourage moss and algae for a mellow 'old' look. Other options include clay or stone edging tiles, logs driven into the ground or dwarf wooden-stake palisades.

Managing beds   Dividing the garden into small plots with intervening paths might seem a waste of growing space, but if made very fertile the beds will yield more produce than widely spaced rows because plants can be grown closer together. This has cultural benefits: crops reach a usable size sooner and their canopy of leaves rapidly covers bare soil, shading out weeds and preventing moisture loss in hot weather. A cropping plan is essential (see page 20).

TIMBER EDGING

The classic potager   A potager is a formal geometric arrangement of small beds where crops are laid out like bedding plants to make an ornamental garden. This traditional French style has been revived as a charming way to fit edible plants into today's small plots without sacrificing artistry. All kinds of crops, including flowers, may be grown together in a potager and organized for visual appeal. A preliminary plan is essential, both to achieve formal balance and harmony and to ensure that the process of harvesting crops does not spoil the precision of the design.

Potager beds are usually small and simple in shape – but not necessarily square or rectangular – and the overall geometry should be kept simple, especially in very small gardens. Incorporating an attractive centrepiece will pull the symmetrical design together and create a strong focal point. This may take the form of a statue, a bed with a central fruit tree or topiary bay, an architectural crop like globe artichokes or angelica, or a wigwam of runner beans.

Between the tall centrepiece and the edging or 'frame', you can plant up the body of the bed with vegetables and salad crops. Space plants fairly close together (see individual entries) and, if possible, fill each bed in one go, using no more than two or three contrasting crops. The aim is to create blocks of colour, form and texture with the impact of seasonal bedding. Combinations might include alternate green and crimson rows of carrots and beetroot, lettuces interplanted with leeks, curly kale undersown with red chicory, or sweet corn grown in a carpet of bush tomatoes or golden courgettes. Remember that a potager is as much for display as for production, and harvesting plants can leave gaps – hence the importance of a clear plan for succession.

EDGING THE BEDS

Defining the outline of beds creates a neat and tidy finish. Potager beds are often edged with dwarf hedges, preferably evergreen, to provide colour and interest in winter. Dwarf box (*Buxus sempervirens* 'Suffruticosa'), shown below, is traditional and may be clipped to a strict outline, but look out for slugs and snails. Evergreen herbs like hyssop, rosemary, catmint and lavender are other options, or you might prefer to plant seasonal edgings of marigolds, cornflowers, nasturtiums, coloured lettuces, parsley or violas. More rigid edging can be provided by treated timber boards nailed to short pegs (opposite). Apples and pears trained as stepover trees (single espaliers), 38cm (15in) high, make a productive edging fence.

THE CONTAINER GARDEN

Containers play an invaluable role in the chef's garden. Not only are they essential where ground space is severely limited or non-existent, but they also offer scope for imaginative placing and composition in the open garden. Whether used singly – strategically sited as focal points or ornamental flourishes – or grouped together as a well-composed collection of plants, containers supply mobile living accommodation while being highly decorative features in their own right.

Choosing containers The enormous range of containers offered to gardeners is extended even further if you include recycled and improvised containers: anything which holds an adequate volume of compost and keeps it moist enough to support healthy root growth can be used. For large containers, consider using barrels, dustbins and troughs (see the Chef's Roof Garden, page 39). Containers fall into two types, depending on their purpose: those used for sowing and growing young plants on during their early stages, and more permanent containers used to house perennial plants for several years.

The purely functional container for raising plants is usually a small pot of full depth or less (half-pots or pans). You will probably accumulate a stock as you introduce new plants to the garden but, to start with, buy several 8–10cm (3–4in) pots for sowing large seeds or for pricking out seedlings, together with a selection of 13-, 15- and 17-cm (5-, 6- and 7-in) diameter pots for potting on developing plants. They may be made from clay, which drains well, or plastic, in which the compost stays moist for longer.

Larger containers are made from a variety of materials. Stone is cool, both in its appearance and the effect it has on rooting conditions, but it is often

VERSATILE CONTAINERS

Containers can be used to transform any soil-less area into a garden. You can green a rooftop with pots, bins and troughs used on a firm surface or hung from walls and fences (opposite). Chimney pots and the deep clay pots known as long toms are suitable for trailing plants. Large recycled wooden boxes treated with preservative will hold permanent plants, such as asparagus. Even an old tyre will hold enough compost for salads and herbs.

TYRE

WOODEN BOX

CHIMNEY POT

LONG TOM

Herbs that are in constant demand
should be grown near the kitchen, and
containers are ideal for this purpose.
The herbs may be kept as potted
specimens in a staged display (below),
but are equally happy massed together
in larger containers, such as the sage,
thyme, parsley and rosemary in the
window box shown opposite.

expensive and very heavy, something to avoid when gardening on a roof or balcony. Glazed terracotta holds moisture as efficiently as plastic, while unglazed clay is porous and, if combined with plenty of drainage material at the base, can prevent the risk of waterlogging and stagnation in wet weather. Make sure pots are frost-resistant if they are to stand outdoors all year, and paint the underside with clear varnish or enamel to prevent them staining the surface on which they stand.

Wood is used for window boxes and for large, square Versailles boxes. It drains well and weathers to an appealing finish, but should always be coated with preservative for durability. Metal containers, especially lead, can last for many years, although iron and steel will eventually rust unless galvanized. Plastics rarely harmonize sympathetically with their surroundings but have the merit of retaining moisture for longer than wood or clay; you can always line porous containers with polythene perforated in places at the base for drainage.

Plants for containers   Almost any plant will thrive in the confines of a suitable container, provided you can satisfy its basic cultural needs. The main requirement is that a pot must hold enough compost to sustain healthy unchecked growth, preferably for a full season. Some plantings will be relatively short-lived – basil in its many forms, leaf lettuce for frequent cutting, or pot marigolds with their brilliant edible flowers – and these may be grown in small pots grouped together to add seasonal colour and interest to corners of sitting areas. Small pots also suit herbs in constant use, such as parsley and chives, and can be rotated so that some recover from being cropped while others are in use. They may be brought indoors for windowsill harvest, or plunged in outdoor window boxes in an inert material like composted bark; when exhausted after cropping, another pot is simply slotted in its place.

At the other extreme, fruit trees eventually need generous-sized containers such as dustbins, wooden boxes, recycled oil drums or deep planters made from a variety of materials such as galvanized steel or terracotta. The larger volume of compost they hold will sustain a community of plants such as a clipped mophead bay or a timber tripod for cucumbers, perhaps underplanted with dwarf spring bulbs and surrounded in summer by golden or purple dwarf beans, edged with trailing petunias or nasturtiums.

Explore the potential of unconventional containers. A strawberry tower would accommodate a complete green salad of mixed lettuces, chicory and endive or a permanent collection of different thymes for a sunny spot where the flowering plants cascade down the sides. Bush cherry tomatoes or young herbs can be grown in an attractive pan or trough, close to an eating area.

THE RIGHT COMPOST

To give container-grown crops the best start, choose good-quality, fresh compost of an appropriate kind. One of the advantages of containers is that you can vary the soil type for the particular plant, using an ericaceous or rhododendron mix for acid-loving crops like blueberries, for example. Soil-based mixtures are easy to manage and tend to tolerate over- or underwatering but they are heavy, a drawback in window boxes or large containers which you many want to move under cover in the winter. Where weight is important, such as on a roof garden, use the lighter soil-less composts (preferably peat-free to help conserve dwindling supplies); do not compress these mixtures too firmly when filling pots, and keep them evenly moist all season as they are difficult to re-wet once dry. For guidance on making compost, see page 138.

THE VERTICAL GARDEN

A garden without height is only a mosaic on the ground, viewed in an instant and lacking three-dimensional impact. By bringing into play the walls and fences that enclose most gardens, you can balance the geometry of the flat plan with a lively vertical presence. You will also increase the potential growing area by as much as one-third, an invaluable gain in the small garden. Growing tall plants as internal divisions as well as exploiting plant supports reinforces the impression that every part of the garden is earning its keep.

Plants for height   The tallest food plants are tree fruits, which can provide perennial height for a generation or more. Apples and pears may be trained as fans and espaliers on house or garden walls, furnishing attractive blossom in spring, autumn fruit and a balanced pattern of bare branches in winter. You can also position them as freestanding accents in the open garden: judicious pruning and training will allow light through to crops growing underneath. Keep your choice of tree in proportion with the rest of the garden – apples, for example, are grafted on various rootstocks which offer heights from 1.8m (6ft) to 9m (30ft) or more. At a lower level, standard-trained soft fruit like goose-berries and red- and whitecurrants are charming and productive features; grown as fans or cordons on wires or trellis, currants and raspberries make excellent fruiting fences and screens up to 1.5m (5ft) high.

For seasonal height, grow climbing and twining vegetables on tripods or obelisks placed as focal points within beds to economize on space; there they will lightly shade lettuces and other leaf crops from hot summer sunlight, and lift your eye above ground level. Tall peas, beans and squashes are all suitable for growing up tripods, and may be combined with annual flowers such as morning glories or sweet peas. Self-supporting crops like sweet corn and Jerusalem artichokes provide seasonal shade and wind protection, and can be used as screening in summer. Tomatoes look luscious and inviting grown as cordons on canes in the open, or trained to climb against walls and fences.

Providing support   Climbers and trained plants need to have their stems held in position. Fix netting, wooden trellis or parallel wires spaced about 30cm (12in) apart to walls and fences with wedge-shaped wall nails driven into mortar joints, or with threaded vine-eyes (you need to drill and plug walls for these), or drive 'lead' wall nails into joints for temporary support. Unless they twine naturally, tie stems in place with soft tarred string and use bamboo canes or larch poles to guide woody branches precisely.

CLIMBING CROPS

Secure climbers to wires stretched between posts or erect a support structure. Bamboo canes are strong enough to support runner beans on wigwams (opposite), or in continuous rows (below); rustic poles are more fitting for cottage gardens. Use twiggy hazel sticks to support peas. Plain or ornate metal structures are available in many designs: they are durable and have a light, airy presence that is less dominating in small gardens. Similar structures were a classic feature of Versailles boxes.

SEATING AND EATING

A chef's garden is somewhere in which to linger, a place full of promise and an invitation to taste and handle the growing plants, so it is fitting to include gathering areas in your design. Define an eating area with pleasing floor materials – weathered bricks or bark for informality, or contrasting paving, stone slabs and even mosaic for a more formal feel. Placing an outdoor dining table close to a raised bed of culinary herbs enables guests to serve themselves with fresh seasonings, while a bench in a corner is good for toasting the setting sun after an evening tending your plants.

A seat outdoors is the most natural place to relax and enjoy the garden. It may be a permanent fixture, blending into the layout, or it could be a portable chair to bring under cover in winter: choose one which is durable, decorative and fits the surroundings. Timber is a natural material that ages gracefully: make sure it comes from a renewable source and is treated to withstand the weather. Wicker seats hint at gentle ease and lazy afternoons, but are only for dry weather. In larger gardens, several seats made of more permanent materials such as brick, stone or rustic timber may be built in, against a wall or by a pool perhaps, or constructed on top of a low wall capped with stone slabs or planted with creeping thyme and Corsican mint to make a classic scented herb seat.

Cooking outdoors is a natural extension of entertaining al fresco, and a barbecue is a desirable outdoor feature. Build a permanent fixture from brick or stone, or use a portable or wheeled barbecue where space is limited. Any kind would be quite at home in the kitchen-garden environment, especially if crops such as sweet corn or asparagus are grown – when cooked within minutes of harvest they retain all their delicious but often fleeting flavours and their preparation near the table can add an extrovert flourish to the occasion.

DINING OUT

Outdoor eating areas need to be furnished and detailed as thoughtfully as any interior design. They can be formal or intimate, depending on your lifestyle, and the area where people gather, such as a terrace, should be planned simply to cater for all occasions. Garden size and layout might allow you to choose between staying close to the house or flat for access to the kitchen, or finding seclusion further away. Whatever you choose, try to match the style of the garden so that table and chairs become an organic part of your design, rather than an imitation of indoor furniture. Where weight is a consideration – such as on balconies and rooftops (opposite) – wirework, cast aluminium or tubular steel is light and resilient.

TOOLS AND EQUIPMENT

Enthusiasts often accomplish a whole range of garden tasks with their bare hands, but a few basic tools are essential for some jobs and make light work of most others. Even if your garden is simply a collection of pots or a window box, you will probably find secateurs, a hand fork and trowel, and a watering can indispensable. In the open kitchen garden efficient irrigation, composting, forcing and protection all depend on your having the appropriate equipment.

Essential tools   A simple kit of well-made comfortable tools will meet most gardening needs and be a pleasure to use. Start with the basic equipment and add others as the need arises; with careful maintenance and storage they should all last a lifetime. For cultivating open ground you will need a good garden fork and a spade. Test them for weight and balance before buying; you may prefer the small lightweight border types over larger traditional models. There is usually a choice of T- or D-shaped handles, and long and short shafts, sometimes angled for extra leverage. Stainless-steel models are expensive but easier to use and keep clean, especially if your ground is sticky. In a larger garden you might invest in a rake and a hoe, but you can often improvise with a fork or spade for levelling, loosening weeds and marking out.

A hand fork is invaluable for weeding, cultivating and lifting plants, and can be fitted with a short handle for close work or a longer one to extend your reach – some models allow you to fit handles of various lengths to the same detachable head. You will also need a trowel for making holes and moving plants: test for comfort by holding it like a dagger (the easiest way to dig a hole) as well as more conventionally like a scoop. Both tools are useful for confined work in pots, growing bags and other containers.

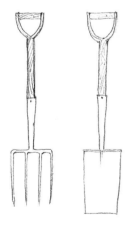

Find space in your collection of essential equipment for pieces of glass, plastic and fleece, which can be used to cover vulnerable plants when temperatures drop dangerously low. Purpose-made covers, such as this modern, unbreakable version of the classic Victorian handlight (left), are versatile aids: they are used for routine frost protection and also for forcing early crops, speeding germination or enclosing cuttings to assist rooting.

For pruning and training fruit trees and bushes, as well as for trimming perennial herbs such as bay, you need a stout pair of secateurs. Both anvil secateurs, with a blade closing against a notch in the opposing jaw, and by-pass models, which operate like scissors, will do the job if they have good-quality cutting edges that are kept regularly sharpened. As with all small tools, it is a good idea to choose models with brightly painted handles so that they are conspicuous if left out in the garden.

Watering equipment Irrigation is an important seasonal task, both in the open garden during summer and throughout the year for containers. A can is essential, preferably with a long spout for convenient watering among pots, and with fine and coarse roses or sprayheads. In larger gardens a hosepipe can save time and effort – do not fit it with a sprinkler, which is indiscriminate and wasteful. It is better to spot-water plants individually, or to couple porous trickle pipes to the hose to deliver water where it is needed. If you can, store rainwater in butts and tanks to reduce the demand on mains services and provide your plants with untreated water at the right temperature.

The garden store Garden tools need to be kept under cover. A weather-proof chest or cupboard is large enough for basic tools, together with the inevitable accumulation of pots, trays, compost and canes, and is certainly the

best solution for very small gardens. Where space permits, a shed can be an architectural asset as well as a practical solution to storing larger tools – and even fruit and vegetables if the inside can be kept frost-free. Nothing beats hanging your garden tools neatly on an inside wall of your shed. Thoughtful choice of design and structure as well as careful positioning help integrate a shed into the garden; it can be covered with climbers such as runner beans or grapes trained on trellis or canes. Some styles combine storage with the additional features of a summerhouse or partial glazing for use as a greenhouse.

Growing under glass In a fickle climate, any kind of protection is valuable for sheltering vulnerable crops from the effects of frost and wind. Small numbers of plants can be raised from seed or cuttings on an indoor windowsill, where pots of herbs and seedling salads may also be kept over winter. Early progress can be made outside by using glass or plastic cloches and handlights to keep a couple of degrees of frost at bay, and to help indoor transplants adjust to open-air conditions. Their shrewd deployment early and late in the year can extend the growing season by two to three weeks at each end.

A small greenhouse or conservatory is the ultimate sanctuary against the weather: all the benefits of a cold frame or cloches are possible here, with the bonus of being able to work inside in comfort and raise some plants to maturity in the extra height available. A conservatory can always double as a sunroom and intermediate dining area between house and garden. A greenhouse will take up more space than other kinds of protection but can be placed carefully in the garden – running east to west and well away from the shade of buildings and nearby trees – to make the most of the light. A propagator, whether heated or not, and automatic ventilation to save frequent adjustment in changeable weather are valuable greenhouse accessories.

STORING FRUIT

Only store or preserve perfect, unblemished fruit and freeze and bottle the same day as picking. Store apples and pears in a frost-free place such as a shed. Lay out apples on newspaper on shelves, not touching each other, or wrap and pack in boxes. Store pears in boxes or on shelves in a little more warmth than apples. Check both crops regularly, pears every few days for approaching ripeness.

the Chefs four poster Vegetable Garden

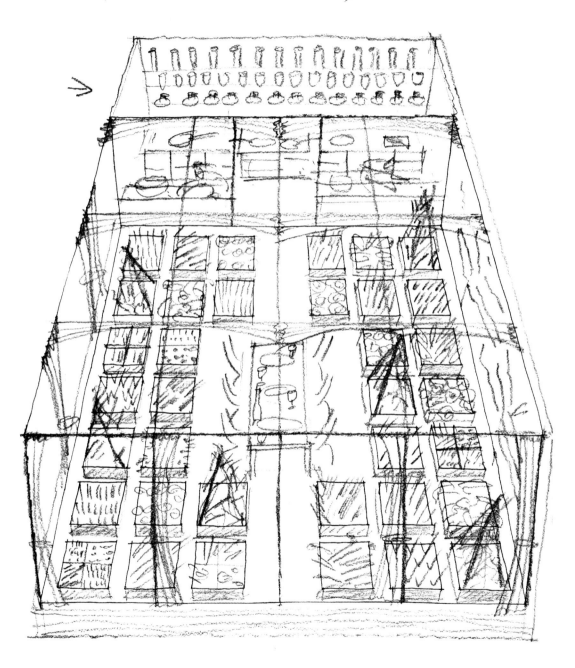

THE CHEF'S ROOF GARDEN

In our restaurants, we are constantly searching for growers who can supply herbs, vegetables and fruit that have real flavour. Usually the produce has to be organically grown and of dependably good quality, and it is equally important that they are reliable. All chefs know this is what they have to demand if they are to deliver consistently good food to their customers.

The Chelsea garden   Our Evening Standard/Laurent Perrier Chef's Roof Garden, exhibited at the 1999 Chelsea Flower Show in London, is designed to satisfy the need for freshness and flavour in an intimate space, about the same size as the average garden of a terraced house. The distances involved and the amount of time elapsing between harvesting, preparing and serving are reduced to an absolute minimum, comparable to gathering home produce just before it is needed in the kitchen. The idea behind the design is to persuade visitors that they can raise excellent produce in any smallish back garden or

THE FOUR-POSTER BED
The garden as a whole can be curtained off with fine, translucent and rot-free curtains running on a metal framework to cover the top and open sides of the growing space (above). Gardeners are increasingly using one or two thicknesses of horticultural fleece to cover or screen crops, and we have extended this idea to create a practical conceit which would provide the chef's garden with shade in summer and protection from frost or wind chill during winter and spring. The overall effect is that of a giant four-poster bed.

FRONT VIEW OF KITCHEN

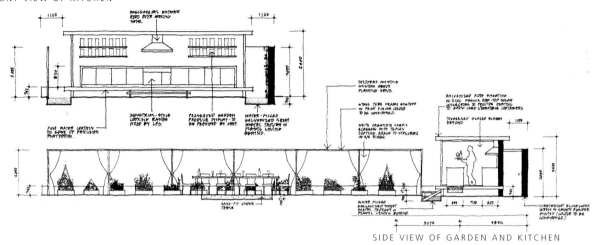

SIDE VIEW OF GARDEN AND KITCHEN

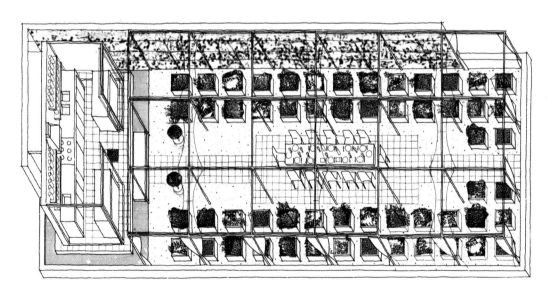

THREE-DIMENSIONAL PLAN

even on a roof terrace. Here, all the crops are growing in large, galvanized metal containers which are fitted with under-soil heating cables to encourage early growth during the cooler part of the season. In addition, a trickle irrigation system has been installed to conduct water direct to the plants and avoid unnecessary waste. The range of produce grown here includes about 100 of the best-flavoured varieties of vegetables, herbs and fruit, many of which are seldom found in the market, but which nonetheless illustrate the variety that can be achieved by cultivating a relatively small space.

THE EXPANDABLE PLAN

The grid of metre-square galvanized troughs (below) can be extended or reduced to exploit the size and shape of any site. The network of intervening paths – made of brick, stone and pebbles – allows easy access to the beds from all sides and to the central seating area.

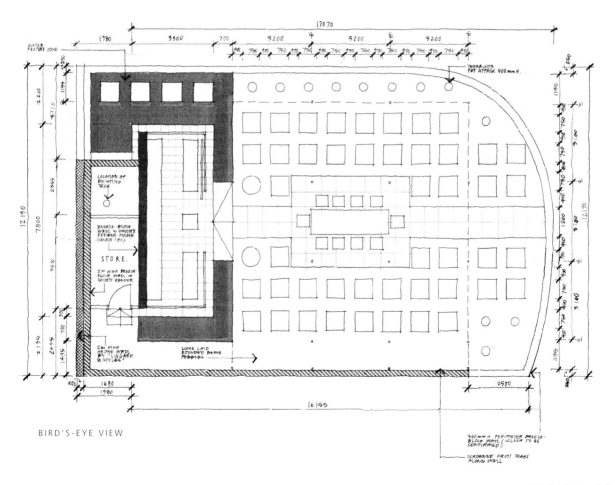

BIRD'S-EYE VIEW

vegetables

With imaginative planning, the small garden can become a cornu-copia of pleasure. Sun-warmed tomatoes fresh from the vine; squashes of all shapes and colours; peas and beans that burst with juice and crispness; sweet corn and asparagus to plunge in boiling water within minutes of harvest – all these are possible from a small plot of soil, a collection of terrace pots or even a rooftop container.

When you grow your own produce, you can gather it in peak condition, before any of its flavour and nutritional value has had a chance to disperse. Choice is another incentive: you can pick unusual and superb-tasting varieties unavailable in supermarkets. Also, if you wish, you can grow vegetables in a totally organic way, without chemical sprays and additives of any kind.

As well as providing fresher, better-tasting vegetables, growing your own will inspire exploration, both culinary and aesthetic. Many vegetables are handsome, and the chef's garden is a place to be imaginative with plants. An ornamental potager needs only a few square metres of ground, while a simple window box can hold a composition of colourful leaf crops such as spinach, ruby chard and beetroot, with an edging of carrots, spring onions and parsley.

KOHL RABI 'Azure Star'

PLANNING AND CHOOSING

Decisions about what to grow are best made at an early stage. There are inventive techniques for squeezing more produce than you might expect from a small space: a 3m (10ft) square patch can provide a family with something to eat all year round; planted intensively, a salad bed 2.5 x 1m (8 x 3ft) will yield a seemingly inexhaustible crop of lettuces. But sooner or later the inevitable limitations of a small garden will challenge you to be selective.

Maincrop vegetables – potatoes, onions and carrots, swedes and parsnips, for example – demand too much space, and good-quality supplies can usually be bought at reasonable prices. So forget them and concentrate instead on more elusive varieties: red onions, miniature parsnips and leeks and finger carrots out of season are all a revelation when grown and served freshly picked. Fast-growing crops such as salad leaves, radishes and kohl rabi take up little space – harvested while still young and in peak condition, they are soon cleared to make way for something else. Vegetables for gathering regularly over a long period are good value, and courgettes, runner beans, mangetout peas and spinach all deserve priority. Cut-and-come-again and seedling salad crops can be prolific, even at close spacings, and specially bred compact or miniature varieties save space. Prime candidates for your cropping scheme should also include any which deteriorate and lose their flavour unless eaten soon after being picked or pulled.

Fitting it all in   Without a coherent plan, there is a danger of sowing too much at once and filling the garden with a glut of vegetables. Pace your sowings throughout the season, bearing in mind that some crops – like leeks and brassicas – take a long time to develop, whereas early varieties of beetroot, lettuce and spinach sprint to maturity and may be grown as 'catch crops', to be harvested and cleared before the slower ones need planting out; keep these in pots and trays while they queue for room. Never leave space idle: keep a back-up supply of successional sowings started in advance, so you have follow-on crops to plant out as soon as the ground is free.

Cooperate with the weather and the aspect of your garden. Make the earliest sowings in the warmest spots or containers in the sun, and use cloches, handlights or horticultural fleece to warm the ground elsewhere to speed germination and growth. Tall or trailing varieties can be trained on vertical supports, leaving precious room below for less vigorous or shade-loving crops, and any needing shelter from wind or frost.

CROP ROTATION

Kitchen gardening books usually include guidance on rotating crops, which involves moving particular groups such as roots or legumes (peas and beans) regularly round the garden to avoid a local build-up of pests, diseases and nutrient imbalances. This advice is often complicated, unnecessarily so for small, intensive gardens. If you simply avoid growing any crop (apart from perennials) in the same place over two consecutive seasons, you should prevent pests and disease problems from occurring.

SOWING METHODS

Most vegetables respond to the same basic sowing routine – sowing, thinning or pricking out and transplanting. Timing can be critical and it is important to become familiar with the seasonal rhythm of raising vegetables, both during and out of their normal season of growth. There are alternative ways to grow

SOWING OUTDOORS

Sow root crops where they are to grow, others in a nursery bed or container for later transplanting – but beware of them running to seed in a hot summer. Wait until the soil is warm (cover the bed with cloches or plastic for 1–2 weeks in cold weather) and not too wet; in dry conditions, water the soil first.
1 Scuffle the surface with a hoe to kill weeds and loosen a fine tilth.
2 Rake the bed level, removing weeds and larger stones. **3** Using a line or cane, mark out shallow parallel furrows. **4** Sow seeds sparingly, spacing larger ones to avoid later thinning. Cover with soil and firm.

1

2

a crop – vegetables entries may suggest sowing direct then thinning, or sowing indoors, and both methods can be used, according to the time of year.

Pricking out   Give seedlings more space to develop when they have two true leaves and are big enough to handle. Water, and allow to drain, then loosen roots with a table fork. Holding each seedling by a leaf, transfer to pots of potting compost – use 8–9cm (3–3½in) pots for large seedlings, trays for small ones, spacing 5cm (2in) apart. Water and keep in a well-lit place.

Thinning   Seedlings sown direct will emerge too crowded, so pull up or lightly fork up unwanted seedlings, leaving the rest at recommended distances; surplus non-root crop seedlings can often be transplanted elsewhere.

3

4

SOWING IN POTS

Sow early and successional crops in small pots or seed trays while waiting for space or warmer weather. Using fresh, moist seed compost, fill containers to the brim and tap to settle. Sprinkle seeds sparingly on the surface, cover with a thin layer of compost (for certain seeds such as celery and celeriac, perlite or vermiculite is better), and stand in a warm place indoors or a shady spot outside in summer. Keep evenly moist during germination.

Transplanting   Seedlings pricked out in containers or sown in a nursery bed are transplanted to their final sites before they get too large; water an hour or two beforehand. Lift outdoor plants with a trowel, without disturbing the rootball; plants in pots are gently tapped out, those in trays eased free with a trowel or separated with a sharp knife. Plant in holes made with a trowel or dibber, firm into place with your fist or fingers, and water thoroughly.

FLOWERING AND FRUITING CROPS

Vegetables which produce flowers or fruits are generally warm-weather crops that need several weeks' fast active growth before plants reach the harvesting stage. Cauliflowers and sprouting broccoli are hardy exceptions, but they occupy the ground for much longer before maturity. As a rule, the larger the plant the heavier its crop, so water and feed regularly to sustain growth.

PURPLE SPROUTING BROCCOLI 'Rudolf'

CAULIFLOWER *Brassica oleracea* Botrytis Group

Full-size white cauliflowers spend months growing and are hard to justify in small gardens, but coloured varieties and miniature cauliflowers, seldom found in shops or only at a high price, are a good choice. Summer cauliflowers grown close together produce miniature heads of tightly packed buds for individual servings. Coloured varieties produce larger heads of lime-green or purple florets.

Cauliflowers revel in the cool, light shade at the foot of runner beans or beside fruit trees and bushes; miniature varieties are arranged in blocks, in large deep pots and boxes, or in deep beds, perhaps interplanted with leeks. They are greedy plants, needing plenty of water and fertilizer throughout their growth. Add a sprinkle of lime beforehand if your ground is acid.

Sow coloured autumn varieties in a tray or seedbed in late spring, thin to 5cm (2in) apart, and transplant 45cm (18in) apart when six weeks old. Grow miniatures 15cm (6in) apart each way: sow from mid-spring to midsummer to head up 10–12 weeks later. Harvest large heads while still tight, miniature varieties when 8–10cm (3–4in) across, then uproot the plant for composting.

White miniature varieties are 'Alpha', 'Dok', 'Snowball', 'Predominant', 'Garant', and 'Perfection'. Coloured autumn kinds include 'Minaret' (lime green, pointed florets), 'Alverda' and 'Limelight' (soft green), 'Purple Queen' (purple).

SPROUTING BROCCOLI *Brassica oleracea* Italica Group

This is a superb spring vegetable, available when others are scarce. Supermarket purple sprouting broccoli is often tired and dehydrated and has lost its flavour, while its cousin, white sprouting, is rarely sold. Both should be gathered young for immediate use to retain their melting texture and delicate taste.

Well-grown plants can reach 1m (3ft) tall and wide, and just one specimen in a large pot will yield a prolific succession of leafy sideshoots from midwinter to mid-spring. Treat like cauliflowers, but make a single sowing in mid-spring to transplant firmly in midsummer, 60cm (2ft) apart. Water in dry weather, and stake in exposed gardens. Cut sideshoots when 10cm (4in) long.

'Rudolf' is one of the first to crop, followed by 'Claret'. 'Purple Sprouting' and 'White Sprouting' come in early and late selections to spread the harvest.

PURPLE SPROUTING BROCCOLI WITH CHILLI AND ANCHOVY

Delicious as it is, as a sauce for pasta or served with a grilled steak. Serves 4

1kg/2lb purple sprouting broccoli
50g/2oz salted anchovies
2 fresh red chillies
4 garlic cloves, peeled and sliced
50ml/2fl oz olive oil

Wash the broccoli, trimming and removing any tough or excess stalks. Rinse and carefully fillet the anchovies and finely chop the chillies. Warm the oil in a heavy-bottomed pan, then add all the ingredients except for the broccoli. Cook very slowly for about 30 minutes. When it is almost completely melted, add the broccoli and cover the pan. Steam for about 10 minutes, until the stalks are tender, and remove the lid. Boil away any excess liquid and serve.

There are many different varieties of
sweet pepper: try a mixture of colours
such as 'Carnival' or 'Bell Boy', 'New
Ace' or 'Slim Pim' (long and narrow);
small-fruited 'Baby Belle' is a prolific
windowsill variety. Varieties of chilli
range from mild 'Crespin', 'Hungarian
Wax' and 'Red Cherry' to the
incendiary 'Jalapeño' and 'Habañero'.

CALABRESE   *Brassica oleracea* Italica Group

Calabrese, or broccoli, is a delicious Mediterranean green vegetable, related to cauliflowers and sharing their fresh succulence, creamy after cooking or crunchy when raw. After harvesting the heavy central head of tight buds, either discard the plants or leave to produce a secondary crop of small leafy flower shoots, rather like a green sprouting broccoli – these are excellent lightly steamed.

Calabrese enjoys similar sites and conditions to cauliflowers, but tolerates lower fertility and moisture levels. Sow 2–3 seeds 30cm (12in) apart and thin to the strongest seedling, or sow as for cauliflowers and transplant after six weeks. Sow from early spring until midsummer for crops three months later. Feed after cutting the main head if you are leaving plants to produce secondary shoots.

Space 'Corvet' as close as 23cm (9in) apart; 'Trixie' grows fast and tolerates club root disease; the dwarf 'Broccoletto' is fast-growing and sweetly flavoured. 'Romanesco' has lime-green heads of conical florets; 'Red Lion' is purple.

PEPPERS   *Capsicum annuum*

Peppers are bushy plants up to 1m (3ft) high and wide. There are two distinct kinds, both rich in vitamin C. Sweet peppers are generally fat and blocky (a few are long and slim), in a range of colours from red, through orange, yellow and green, to lilac, black and white – brighter-coloured varieties are the sweetest. After removing their seeds, whole peppers can be roasted or stuffed; or the thick walls cut into strips for use raw or cooked. Hot peppers or chillies range in pungency from warm and mellow to blisteringly fiery, and are widely used in savoury South American, Asian, Romanian and Mediterranean dishes. Along with tomatoes, peppers exhibit a great difference in flavour between the handsome but tasteless mass-grown varieties and those you have raised yourself in the sun.

All peppers love full sun and heat, and are best grown in clay pots under glass or in a sheltered corner of a terrace. To fruit well outdoors, they like the protection of cloches or a cold frame in all but the most favoured gardens. Buy young plants in late spring for potting up in 10–13cm (4–5in) pots, or sow in late winter, germinating the seeds at 21°C (70°F); reduce the temperature to 15°C (60°F) once they emerge. Transfer at the three-leaf stage to 8cm (3in) pots and move on to larger pots as they develop. Peppers thrive on restricted root growth, so aim to end up with single plants in pots no bigger than 20–23cm (8–9in). Alternatively, harden off and plant out after the last frosts, 45cm (18in) apart.

Pinch out growing tips when plants are 38cm (15in) high. Water regularly, especially during flowering and fruiting, and spray the flowers with tepid water in the evenings to help them set. Feed with liquid fertilizer every 7–10 days when fruits start swelling. Fruits take 60–100 days to mature: picking sweet peppers while still green encourages further crops, or they may be left to turn colour. Freeze surplus peppers whole or sliced. Leave chillies to ripen on the plants, but pick while still bright and glossy – to store, string them on thread and leave to dry in a warm place for 1–2 weeks. Hang over the stove for constant use or keep them in tightly sealed plastic bags in the refrigerator – or grind in a spice mill.

CUCUMBER *Cucumis sativus*

The smooth-skinned cucumber found in shops is a tropical climber that needs heat and humidity, and only does well under glass with vigilant pest and disease control. The fruits can reach 60cm (2ft) long and are usually eaten raw in salads. Cultivation methods can be found in a specialist greenhouse handbook.

You are more likely to succeed with ridge cucumbers, hardier outdoor plants that mostly produce slightly warty, short green fruits. There are also round apple-shaped or long slim Japanese kinds, which grow well in warm shade and make lush 1.8-m (6-ft) tall highlights when the trailing stems are tied to trellis or tripods. If their tough skins are peeled, the fruits can be used like greenhouse cucumbers, or you can pick them while still small for brining or pickling.

Sow in small pots in gentle heat 5–6 weeks before the last frosts, setting two seeds on edge in each pot. Retain the stronger seedling, keep warm and pot on if necessary. Harden off and plant out after the frosts, 45–60cm (18–24in) apart, in fertile soil or in 30cm (12in) pots of rich compost. Pinch out growing tips after 5–6 leaves and tie sideshoots to supports. Water frequently (avoid leaves) and feed weekly once fruits form. Harvest when fruits are a usable size – regular picking encourages more to develop. Varieties include 'Burpless Tasty Green', 'Kyoto' and 'Tokyo Slicer' (long, slim), 'Bush Champion' (shrubby) and 'White Wonder'.

CUCUMBER 'Telegraph Improved'

SQUASH VARIETIES

The huge, exciting range of squashes comprises two main kinds. Summer squashes, such as courgette (zucchini), marrow, custard marrow and spaghetti squash, are eaten as soon as they are ready. Marrows, often grown to monstrous size and stored for winter, are best harvested when small or medium. Winter squashes, such as pumpkins, acorn, butternut and Hubbard squash have tough skins, and store for months. 'Ambassador', 'Gold Rush' (yellow), 'Taxi' (yellow), 'Rondo de Nice' (round) are all excellent courgette varieties. Marrows include 'Tiger Cross', 'Zebra Cross' and 'Long Green Trailing'. Other summer kinds include 'Custard White' (pattypan or custard squash), 'Yellow Crookneck', long, bell-tipped 'Tromboncino' and 'Spaghetti Squash'. Pumpkins and winter squashes include 'Acorn', 'Autumn Giant', 'Butternut', 'Little Gem', 'Red Kuri' and 'Triple Treat' (good seeds for roasting).

COURGETTE 'Rondo de Nice'

SQUASHES   *Cucurbita* species

Squashes are versatile vegetables that can make a real contribution to the chef's garden; all types and varieties are sown and grown in the same way. Plant bushy courgettes and marrows in large containers or as handsome specimens in beds. Trailing kinds are rampant and need careful placing in the small garden: train small-fruited varieties on fences, arches and tripods, where their large yellow flowers and coloured fruits will add an exotic flourish. Allow the larger pumpkins to trail as ground cover under beans, sweet corn and fruit trees, or plant them on the top of compost heaps.

Most squashes can be steamed, sautéed, roasted, stir-fried or deep-fried. Courgettes are good raw and finely sliced, their flowers a delicacy when stuffed or added to risottos. Pumpkins are traditionally made into pies and tarts for Thanksgiving, hollowed out for Hallowe'en and used in Italian cooking. The darker flesh of larger squashes has a distinctive, nutty flavour and is used in soups.

No variety is hardy, so start four weeks before the last frosts by sowing seeds on edge in individual pots. Keep at 15°C (60°F) until the seedlings emerge, then plant out in rich soil or compost, bushy kinds 60cm (2ft) apart, trailers 45cm (18in) if trained as climbers or 1.2m (4ft) for ground cover. Tie in climbing stems with raffia. Water lavishly in dry weather, and feed weekly once fruits appear. Harvest courgettes when 10cm (4in) long with the flowers still attached, marrows while young (8–10 weeks after planting). Leave winter squashes to mature on the plants – firm skins, good colour and dry cracking stalks indicate ripeness. For Hallowe'en pumpkins, pick off all but 2–3 fruits. Cut these with a length of stem attached, keep in full sun for 10–14 days until the skins are hard and the cut stalks sealed, then store on shelves or in nets at 10°C (50°F).

GLOBE ARTICHOKE *Cynara scolymus*

With their long, jagged, silver-grey leaves and fat flowerbuds which open as violet-blue 'thistles', globe artichokes are tall, dramatic plants that deserve to be given space in flower borders, each plant yielding up to 10–12 artichokes of varying size. Plants are perennials of borderline hardiness, growing 60cm–1.8m (2–6ft) high according to variety. They die right down in winter when they are best mulched against frost. They also make handsome seasonal container subjects for sunny, sheltered positions if the pots are insulated or brought under cover in winter; otherwise grow in groups in beds and around fruit trees.

Sow in pots or a cold frame in early spring, and plant out the strongest seedlings after the frosts. Alternatively buy named plants in late spring and set out 60cm (2ft) apart in light or well-drained fertile soil. Water in dry weather and feed every two weeks in summer. In cold winters cover crowns with straw or leaves. Every 3–4 years renew plants by digging up and transplanting young offsets. Cut heads from midsummer to early autumn before their bud scales open.

EATING ARTICHOKES

The tender fleshy base and hearts of the immature flower buds are the parts of an artichoke generally eaten. The bases of the bracts are eaten hot, dipped in butter or hollandaise sauce, while the hearts may be stuffed, baked, fried or used in soups and stews. Tiny whole heads or hearts can be cut in half and fried or cooked and preserved in oil; otherwise artichokes are eaten straight after cutting.

'Green Globe' has the largest buds but it is slightly less hardy than the well-flavoured 'Vert de Laon' or the purple-headed 'Violetto de Chioggia'.

FRAME FOR TOMATOES

TOMATO VARIETIES

For standard size tomatoes, grow 'Harbinger', striped 'Tigerella', 'Ailsa Craig' and 'Craigella'. 'Sungold' (orange), 'Gardeners' Delight' (red) and 'Sun Baby' (yellow) have cherry-like fruits, while 'St Pierre' and 'Mountain Pride' are large-fruited. Bush varieties include 'Red Alert', 'Golden Sunrise', 'Marmande' (large fruits) and 'Roma' (plum variety for pulping). 'Phyra', 'Tumbler' and 'Tiny Tim' are compact bushes for pots and hanging baskets. Explore heritage kinds such as 'Black Russian' (green/black flavour variety), 'Amish Paste' (meaty and tangy, for purée) and 'Broad Ripple Yellow Currant' (golden berries in long trusses).

TOMATOES *Lycopersicum esculentum*

Outdoor tomatoes are an essential ingredient in cooking and deserve to be grown in every chef's garden for their flavour. The choice is vast, ranging from tall large-fruited kinds grown like cordon fruit trees down to miniature bushy varieties perfect for window boxes, containers and hanging baskets. There are red, yellow, green and striped varieties, some as large as apples, others like small cherries or tiny currants. With a little protection from cold and wind, you can extend the range to include Italian plum and meaty French 'beefsteak' tomatoes.

The tomatoes you buy have little of the richness and piquancy of home-grown produce, especially when high-quality, well-flavoured varieties such as 'Marmande', 'St Pierre' and 'Tigerella' are selected. As a fresh, uncooked salad ingredient, the taste of the slowly sun-ripened fruit is supreme; in cooked dishes they are a major culinary flavouring and the basis of many sauces and stews. In high summer there is often a glut of fruit, and this is the time to pulp, juice or sun-dry the surplus for winter use; they may also be bottled or frozen as a purée.

Warmth and plenty of sunshine are the secrets of success, with shelter from chilling winds and draughts. In cold areas, outdoor tomatoes are best grown against a wall or fence or protected in a porch or conservatory; alternatively choose a greenhouse variety and keep under glass at all times. In milder climates grow outdoor kinds in large pots, boxes, growing bags and beds, with tall varieties in rows or decorative groups and bushy types as edging and in containers, much as you would use summer bedding flowers.

Cultivating tomatoes is easier than many gardeners suspect. However, they are not hardy plants and must be raised under glass from seed or bought as growing plants later in the season (but this inevitably restricts choice of variety). For outdoor use, sow about eight weeks before the last frosts, sprinkling the seeds in pans or pots and keeping them at 15–18°C (60–65°F). Prick out at the three-leaf stage into small pots, and pot on into a larger container when these are full of roots. Harden off for planting out when the first flower truss shows, in a frame or under cloches in late spring, or outdoors after the frosts. The ground should be fertile and well-drained, with plenty of humus added to it; mulch after planting to conserve moisture.

TOMATO 'Gardeners' Delight'

Water weekly once flowering begins, and feed container plants with high-potash fertilizer at every watering. Tall ('indeterminate') varieties are tied to canes and their sideshoots pinched out to concentrate growth into a single stem; in late summer, pinch out the growing tip to leave 3–5 trusses of fruit. Trim back some of the lower leaves to two leaf joints to help ripen the fruits; this also improves the circulation of air, which helps to prevent some diseases. Bush ('determinate') kinds of tomato branch naturally and are left unpinched. Pick ripe fruits regularly. When the first frosts threaten, hang complete plants or branches under glass to finish ripening, or spread out the green fruits in a box with a ripe banana or orange to hasten colouring. There are hundreds of tomato varieties and it is worth trying one or two new ones annually (see list opposite).

TOMATO SALAD WITH FISH

Tomatoes of exceptional flavour require nothing more than sea salt, freshly ground pepper and a good olive oil. When their season is in full swing and the myriad varieties and shapes of tomato are all bursting with taste, a salad topped off with some crisp roast fish is sublime. Serves 4

1kg/2lb plum, cherry or tiger-striped
   vine-ripened tomatoes
4 x 225–300g/8–10oz pieces fresh
   fish, such as sea bass or red mullet
salt and freshly ground black pepper
flour for dusting
extra-virgin olive oil
225g/8oz black olives, to garnish
a few basil leaves (optional)
2 lemons, to serve

Preheat oven to 200°C/400°F/Gas 8. If the fish is on the bone, leave it on for easier cooking and better flavour. An hour or so before cooking the fish, cut the tomatoes and arrange prettily on plates. Season with salt and pepper and pour olive oil over them. Lightly dust the fish with seasoned flour. Pour some oil into a heavy ovenproof dish and heat up. Place the fish carefully in the oil and put into the oven for 10 minutes (for fillets) or 20 minutes (on the bone). Place the cooked fish on the tomato salad and drizzle over a little oil. Scatter olives and ripped basil over the top and serve with lemon halves.

BAKED STUFFED AUBERGINES

AUBERGINE   *Solanum melongena*

Classic Mediterranean dishes such as moussaka, ratatouille and caponata depend on aubergines, or eggplants, for their stimulating, slightly pungent flavour. Varieties available to gardeners usually produce plump, black or purple pear-shaped fruits, but other colours and shapes are in cultivation and, if you find some of these as fruits, save the seeds to sow at home. The plants look striking, with large felted leaves, lilac flowers and shiny fruit; they look handsome grouped with peppers and tomatoes. Three or four plants in 20cm (8in) pots should supply a family from midsummer until the frosts. The fat, juicy kinds may be stuffed and baked, while the drier flesh of slim varieties is good fried quickly in olive oil.

Sow and grow like tomatoes (see pages 52–3), and plant out after the frosts, 45cm (18in) apart in fertile, well-drained soil; stand pots in a sunny position. Pinch out growing tips when plants are 30–38cm (12–15in) high to encourage branching, and pinch the ends of branches once 5–6 fruits have set. Strong-growing plants may need staking. Pick fruits while young and shiny, and use immediately or keep for up to a week on a warm shelf. Purée surplus fruits with added sesame-seed tahina paste and garlic, then freeze.

'Black Beauty', 'Enorma' and 'Moneymaker' have large black fruits; 'Vista' fruits are medium-size, those of 'Short Tom' small and early. 'Onita' has long thin fruits, perfect for slicing; 'Bambino' is a miniature 30cm (12in) high, with prolific crops of 2.5cm (1in) fruits. A white variety, 'Ova', is decorative but lacks taste.

SWEET CORN *Zea mays*

Sweet corn's sweetness and flavour start deteriorating less than an hour after harvest, so immediate use is crucial – cobs keep fresh for 2–3 days if stored in plastic bags in the refrigerator. Cobs are boiled or steamed whole, stripped of their husks and tassels, and served with plenty of butter. The tall, robust plants cast little shadow and may be underplanted with squashes or combined with climbing French beans. Grow in decorative blocks or clusters (grouping aids pollination). Each plant yields 1–2 cobs. Baby corn varieties produce several short cobs noted for crispness rather than flavour and used in stir-fries.

In cool gardens, choose early varieties that mature in late summer. Sow seeds individually in small pots, indoors at 15°C (60°F), about six weeks before the last frosts. Harden off thoroughly and plant out 38cm (15in) apart in blocks, baby corn 15cm (6in) apart. Harvest when the silky tassels turn brown and a pressed kernel oozes milky juice. 'Butterscotch' and 'Sweet Nugget' have high sugar levels; 'Champ' and 'Gourmet' retain their sweetness for longer after harvest – grow these kinds away from regular varieties, since cross-fertilization reduces flavour. 'Honey Bantam Bicolour' has yellow and white kernels; 'Minor' produces 4–6 baby cobs, while 'Red Strawberry' is a popcorn variety with tiny red kernels on strawberry-shaped cobs.

BAKED STUFFED AUBERGINES

A half makes a perfect starter and a whole is a meal in itself. This dish is both simple and delicious. Serves 4

4 medium-sized aubergines
175ml/6fl oz olive oil
2 medium onions, sliced
2–3 garlic cloves, peeled and sliced
50g/2oz stoned black olives, halved
50g/2oz salted anchovy fillets, chopped
½ teaspoon chopped fresh thyme
salt and freshly ground black pepper
chopped fresh parsley, to garnish

Preheat oven to 200°C/400°F/Gas 8. Cut the aubergines in half lengthways and score the flesh into squares, taking care not to cut through the skin. Heat a large baking tray and pour on enough olive oil to cover the base. Lay in the aubergines, cut side down, and bake for 20–25 minutes, or until the flesh is golden brown and soft. Leave to cool. In a sauté pan, fry the onions slowly in olive oil until softened. Add the garlic, olives and anchovies to the pan and fry gently for a further 10 minutes. Using a sharp knife, remove the flesh from the aubergines, chop and add to the fried onion mixture, along with some thyme. Season and spoon the mixture back into the scooped-out halves, then return to the oven for 10 minutes. Allow to cool, and strew with parsley before serving.

LEEK VARIETIES

Careful choice of varieties will ensure supplies from midsummer to late spring. The earliest leek varieties are 'King Richard' and 'Hannibal'; for winter use choose 'Musselburgh', 'Longbow' and '(Monstruoso di) Carentan'. 'Kajak', 'Conora' and the blue-leaved 'St Victor' carry crops through the spring. Any variety can be used for miniature leeks: pull when they are the size of spring onions.

L E E K 'Blue Solaise'

LEAVES AND STEMS

These vegetables are often the most adaptable for small gardens and container cultivation. Their productive season can last weeks or months if they are grown at full spacing until maturity, but you can also grow many of them at high density to harvest while still young, sometimes as seedling crops for cutting repeatedly with scissors. This group also includes perennials such as asparagus and seakale. All need fertile soil and plenty of water in dry weather.

LEEK   *Allium porrum*

This hardy, easily grown vegetable is increasing in popularity, along with immature miniature leeks, as slim as spring onions but with the familiar rich melting flavour of the full-size crop. Leeks are classic ingredients of winter soups such as cock-a-leekie and vichyssoise, and a fine vegetable in their own right, steamed, poached in wine or used cold in a variety of ways.

The plants look distinctive, with their fans of long, rich green or steely-blue leaves like broad ribbons, and fat white stems. They can be grown in rows or blocks, in beds and deep containers, and provide an exciting contrast tucked among lettuces, oriental brassicas or flowering plants such as marigolds and rudbeckia. Miniature leeks grow well in window boxes and wide, shallow pans.

Leeks thrive in deep fertile soil, in full sun or shade. Sow early varieties in a cold frame in late winter or early spring, later ones outdoors in mid-spring. Thin seedlings to 2.5cm (1in) apart and, when 15–20cm (6–8in) high, transplant individually into holes 10–15cm (4–6in) deep, made with a dibber. Settle each transplant in place by filling the hole with water. Hand-weed regularly and water in very dry weather; feed early crops every 3–4 weeks for fast growth. Sow miniature leeks direct in rows 8cm (3in) apart, and thin to 2.5cm (1in) apart.

Start harvesting as soon as plants are large enough for use: lift with a fork as needed, trim the leaves and peel off the outer skin for clean white shanks. Before a hard frost several can be lifted and stored in a cool place for a week or so.

Green (or American) celery has naturally
pale green stems with a reasonably
strong flavour, preferred by some to the
mild taste of self-blanching celery, with
white or cream stems.'Victoria' and
'Green Utah' are the best green kinds;
'Celebrity', 'Lathom' and 'Pink
Champagne' are all popular self-
blanching types. 'White Pascal' and
'Clayworth Pink' are well-flavoured
trench varieties, while pale green
'Hopkins Fenlander' may be grown
as a trench or self-blanching variety.
'Iram', 'Monarch' and 'Giant Prague'
are all good celeriac varieties.

SPRING ONION *Allium cepa*

Often called salad onions or scallions, these form slim white stems, with a crisp texture and mild onion flavour. They eventually develop small bulbs, and some varieties with silver-skinned bulbs are grown especially for pickling. All types are used fresh from the garden in salads and omelettes and as an essential ingredient of Chinese and Thai dishes.

Plants need warm, well-drained soil and prefer full sun, but tolerate shade. You can grow them in short rows in beds or boxes, or broadcast the seed evenly in broad shallow pans. Crops grow fast, often maturing about eight weeks from sowing, and may be fitted in as a catch crop between other slower vegetables. Sow little and often, and use while still young.

For spring use, choose a winter-hardy variety and sow direct in late summer. Space rows 10cm (4in) apart and thin seedlings in late winter to 2.5cm (1in) apart. Start summer sowings in early spring, leaving seedlings unthinned until pulled for use; repeat every 3–4 weeks until midsummer for continuous supplies. Water when dry, and hand-weed crops regularly as they detest competition.

The main overwintering variety is 'White Lisbon: Winter Hardy', but 'Guardsman' (a Japanese type) also survives cold weather well, without becoming hot or bulbous. For general use, choose 'Emerald Isle' (long shanks, bright green leaves), 'Redmate' or 'Redbeard' (intensely red stems), 'Purplette' (purple stems) and the traditional 'White Lisbon'. Pickling onions, with their small, hard, silver-skinned bulbs, are grown in the same way; the best variety is 'Barletta'.

CELERY *Apium graveolens*

The taste of celery is unique: nutty and lingering, with a pleasant bitterness that enhances companion flavours. It varies in strength from the aromatic mildness of celeriac to the pungent bite of leaf celery. The best flavoured celery is grown in trenches, earthed up as it grows to blanch its long, crisp stems for winter use. This is hard to accomplish in small gardens, although these varieties may be grown on the surface and blanched in lengths of drainpipe or brown paper sleeves.

To produce the very best sticks for eating raw, water lavishly during growth (celery is originally a bog plant). For cooking, less impressive crops can be just as good including thin-stalked continental varieties which are more like those of the wild plant. The stems and hearts or bases of plants may be used in soups, stews, stuffings and stock; chopped leaves can also be added to cooked dishes.

Fork plenty of compost or similar organic matter in the soil before growing celery, to retain moisture and fuel rapid growth. Plants need a long growing season, so start 10–12 weeks before the last frosts. Sow indoors on the surface of moist compost (the seeds need light to germinate), at about 10°C (50°F). Prick out into trays and grow on under glass until plants have 5–6 true leaves. Harden off and plant out in a warm, sunny spot 15–30cm (6–12in) apart – closer spacing produces smaller plants. Arrange in blocks to improve the blanch of the inner plants, which receive less light. Water generously in dry weather and feed with high-nitrogen liquid fertilizer at every watering from midsummer onwards. Tucking straw between plants helps to produce paler stems. Harvest when plants are large enough: self-blanching kinds from late summer, green varieties from early autumn and trench types a month or so later; use before the hard frosts. Lift with a fork, trim off roots and tops, and discard any split fibrous outer stems.

Leaf celery is a valuable bushy plant grown for repeated cutting for flavouring; one plant is usually sufficient. Any time in spring or summer, sprinkle a pinch of seeds in a small pot and plant out as a clump 5–6 weeks later, or transfer to a 17–20cm (7–8in) pot. Cut leaves as needed from four weeks after planting. Leaf celery is hardy and can be left to produce strongly flavoured seeds for bread.

CELERIAC   *Apium graveolens* var. *rapaceum*

Celeriac is a close relative, sometimes called turnip-rooted celery. The rounded, knobbly edible part is not a root but the swollen 'bulb' at the stem base, with a mild celery flavour. It can be grated raw and mixed with mayonnaise, cooked as a celery substitute or mashed into a purée as an alternative to potatoes.

Plants tolerate poorer conditions than celery, although a little indulgence produces the best bulbs. Grow like celery, and plant out 23–30cm (9–12in) apart in beds, boxes or large pots. Use from mid-autumn when bulbs are 10cm (4in) across. Move containers under cover when frost threatens; open ground crops can be covered with cloches or lifted for storing in boxes of straw or damp sand.

CELERIAC 'Monarch'

ASPARAGUS EGGAH

*The best way to eat asparagus is freshly
steamed, with a bowl of hollandaise.
Adding the cooked stalks to eggs and
baking them, Arab style, in the oven is
also a delicious way to serve it. The cream
is inauthentic but enriching. Serves 6*

32 fresh asparagus spears
12 free-range eggs
salt and freshly ground pepper
pinch of sugar
50g/2oz unsalted butter
100ml/4fl oz cream (optional)
1 teaspoon lemon juice

Preheat oven to 200°C/400°F/Gas 8.
Trim the asparagus and cut each spear
into three lengths. Poach in a little
salted water and drain in a colander.
Beat the eggs in a bowl and season
with salt, pepper and sugar. Melt the
butter in a heavy-bottomed ovenproof
sauté pan. When it foams, add the
eggs, then the asparagus, cream and
lemon juice. Stir for a minute with a
wooden spoon, then place the pan in
the hot oven. Stir the eggah every 7–8
minutes until just set. Allow to sit until
cool enough to cut before serving
with crusty bread.

ASPARAGUS *Asparagus officinalis*

Kitchen gardening books will tell you that asparagus is a luxury crop that
demands a lot of room, but this is no reason to exclude this delicious fern from
the small garden. Plants can be grown as close as 30cm (12in) apart in groups, in
the open ground, in tubs or in raised beds filled with light soil or compost, which
will satisfy their need for good drainage. Outside the cutting season, the tall
feathery plumes of asparagus are an elegant addition to flower borders. The part
eaten is the young shoot or 'spear', cut when 15–20cm (6–8in) high over an
eight-week season and finishing at midsummer, when shoots are allowed to grow
unchecked to restore the plants' energy.

ASPARAGUS EGGAH

Cut spears deteriorate fast, a good reason for growing your own to minimize the time between gathering and cooking. Preparation is simple: trim off the hard ends of spears, wash, steam or poach gently until just tender, and serve with melted butter or an hollandaise-based sauce. Save the fattest spears for this, and use thinner ones ('sprue') to make a delicious soup or omelette filling.

The perennial plants can crop for 30 years or more; two dozen will yield a respectable annual harvest after their second or third year. Grow them in an open sunny position, exposed to winter frosts but sheltered from cold spring winds. Buy one- or two-year-old crowns in early spring, and plant 8–10cm (3–4in) below the surface, 30–45cm (12–18in) apart, with their roots spread out sideways. You can also sow seeds in spring in small pots for planting out the following autumn, but the first harvest will be delayed a further season.

Keep weed-free, and do not cut spears in the first year. Either mulch the plants in autumn with compost or manure, or feed with general fertilizer in early spring and midsummer. In the second year, cut a spear or two from each crown if you like, but wait until the following season before harvesting freely. Use a knife to cut spears just below the surface. Cut down yellowing foliage in autumn.

ORACH *Atriplex hortensis*

This hardy annual has been cultivated in Asia and south-eastern Europe since ancient times. Commonly used as a substitute for spinach, it is also a popular border plant, with its deep red leaves.

While very small, leaves and growing tips can be cut and added to mixed salads for colour and tartness; the larger arrow-shaped leaves are picked for cooking like spinach – they have a similar, though milder, flavour. The slim, single-stemmed plants grow best in moist, light soils and can reach 1.8m (6ft) high, forming elegant spires of dark red, gold or rich green foliage (but leave a few plants to flower and set seed for the following year). From early spring to midsummer, sow seeds in rows in beds and boxes, or sprinkle among shrubs and perennial herbs; make further sowings in a dry season, when plants often run to seed quickly. Pinch out the flowering tips to encourage leaf production. Green, red ('Rubra') and gold forms are all worth growing.

ASPARAGUS VARIETIES

'Connover's Colossal' and 'Martha Washington' are classic green kinds of asparagus, with male and female plants (the latter bear bright red berries in autumn). 'Franklim', 'Venlim', 'Lucullus' and 'Limbras' are all-male varieties with thicker spears. 'Jersey Giant' is prolific, with purple tips, while 'Purple Passion' is deep purple all over (green when cooked). There are also regional variations in culture, mainly between white asparagus, blanched by earthing up the stems, and the more strongly flavoured green asparagus grown on the surface.

LAND CRESS

LAND CRESS   (American cress) *Barbarea verna*

Sometimes known as spring cress or scurvy grass, this reliable watercress substitute is hardy and grows fast. The low bushy plants have a warm, spicy flavour, almost identical to that of watercress (which needs running water to grow well). If sown successively, it can be available all year from shady beds, a cold frame, window boxes or other containers; it is an excellent edging plant, a catch crop to grow between other vegetables, and a windowsill salad for use out of season.

Make monthly sowings from early spring to early summer, and in late summer for winter/spring use. Sow in pots or seed trays, then prick out, or sow direct and thin to final spacings of 15cm (6in) each way. Add plenty of compost to the soil, avoid hot, sunny positions and water regularly in dry weather to prevent plants from becoming bitter. Pick the leaves when large enough, about eight weeks after sowing when plants are 8–10cm (3–4in) high. Harvest regularly to delay flowering and keep plants productive. Only the species is normally grown.

CHARD   *Beta vulgaris* Cicla Group

Swiss chard or seakale beet is related to perpetual spinach and beetroot. Varieties have been developed which produce prolific leaf crops, making chard a most colourful foliage plant. A good choice for potagers and containers, it combines well with blue-tinted plants such as savoy cabbage or borage.

Chard is a dual-purpose vegetable. Its large, glossy green or purplish leaves, deeply sculpted and crinkled, are cooked on their own like spinach. The broad fleshy midribs and stalks – pure white, golden yellow or deep red – have a delicate juicy flavour when steamed or poached in bundles like asparagus. Plants are hardy and yield steadily from late summer until late the following spring.

Chard needs rich, well-manured soil in an open position, away from shade where mildew may occur in damp weather. Sow direct, spacing pinches of seed 30cm (12in) apart each way, thinning to leave the best seedlings, or sow in a seedbed for transplanting. Make a sowing two weeks before the last frosts for use in late summer and winter, and another in late summer for spring and summer cutting the following year. Water in dry weather, especially when young, and mulch to conserve moisture. Pull leaves as needed, a few from each plant.

CHARD VARIETIES
'Burgundy Chard' (purple-red), 'Rhubarb (Ruby) Chard' and 'Charlotte' (both scarlet), and 'Italian' (white-stemmed) are most popular; there are also mixtures of red, yellow and white varieties.

CHARD 'Bright Lights'

GRATIN OF CHARD

Serves 4

1 onion, finely chopped
2 garlic cloves, finely chopped
olive oil
1 fresh red chilli, finely chopped
225g/8oz unsmoked pancetta,
    cut into lardons
salt, freshly ground black pepper
    and nutmeg
1kg/2lb red or green chard
coarsely ground breadcrumbs

Preheat oven to 200°C/400°F/Gas 8.
Fry the onion and garlic gently in a
little olive oil in a large saucepan. When
softened and lightly browned, add the
chilli, along with the pancetta.
Cook slowly for 15 minutes, then
season with salt, pepper and nutmeg.
While this cooks, peel, trim and finely
chop the stalks of the chard and wash
the leaves well. Cook the stalks in
boiling, salted water until tender and
drain thoroughly. Add the stalks to the
onions and fry for a minute, then place
the leaves on top and allow them to
wilt. Put the contents of the pan into a
gratin dish, cover with breadcrumbs
and bake in the hot oven until the
top is lightly crisp.

KALE *Brassica oleracea* Acephala Group

This is one of the hardiest of winter and spring greens, providing a succession of tender young shoots starting in early autumn, with the main season of use from midwinter to mid-spring. The strong and distinctive flavour blends well with pork or bacon, although the leaves can be substituted in any cabbage recipe.

Kale grows like a miniature palm tree, some varieties having curled, crimped or coloured foliage that make exciting highlights in beds – dwarf curly varieties were

CALDO VERDE

once used for decorative winter bedding in potagers. Kale tolerates poorer conditions than most brassicas, but you should always lime acid soils.

Sow in a seedbed or in trays in late spring, prick out or thin to 5cm (2in), and plant out finally 38–45cm (15–18in) apart when about eight weeks old. Water in dry weather, and in early spring feed with high-nitrogen fertilizer. Gather young leaves while still small for adding raw to salads; later they become tough and strong, and it is the new shoots that are harvested when about 10cm (4in) long.

'Dwarf Curled' is best for small gardens; 'Nero di Toscana' (black or Russian kale) has dark crinkly leaves for use from late summer; 'Russian Red' has crimped, purple-red foliage; 'Ragged Jack' is an old variety with serrated, pink-tinted leaves.

CABBAGE *Brassica oleracea* Capitata Group

There is a cabbage type for every season of the year, and growing them all could fill a small garden. Decide which you enjoy the most, or which cannot be bought locally grown in a farmer's field. Winter cabbages demand a lot of space, whereas summer varieties are more compact and do not keep fresh for long, so there is a case for concentrating on these. The intricate, prettily puckered leaves of savoy cabbages are an asset in the winter garden. Red cabbage is handsome and a chef's delight when cooked well, while spring greens or collards (high in vitamins A and C, and calcium) have crisp, juicy loose leaves with a rich flavour.

A sunny position is essential, and the soil needs to be rich and very firm for hearted varieties, with a sprinkle of lime if acid. Most cabbages are unsuitable for containers, where spring greens are more likely to succeed. Always sow in a seedbed or in trays for transplanting when seedlings are 6–8 weeks old, at about 15cm (6in) high. Sow summer varieties from early spring onwards, to mature 12–16 weeks later; plant out 30–35cm (12–14in) apart. Sow autumn and winter kinds in mid- or late spring, for transplanting 45cm (18in) apart, and spring cabbages in late summer, planting out 15–20cm (6–8in) apart. Use alternate plants while still young, leaving the others to grow on to maturity.

Water in dry weather (soak and firm transplants). Harvest plants when large enough by cutting them just below the outer leaves. Pull up winter cabbages before frosts, and keep for 2–3 weeks suspended in a cool, dark place.

CALDO VERDE

This brilliant Portuguese soup is a meal in itself, accompanied simply by some good bread and olives. Serves 6

650g/1½lb curly kale
650g/1½lb potatoes, peeled, cubed
4 garlic cloves, peeled, thinly sliced
100ml/4fl oz olive oil
225g/8oz chorizo sausage, thinly sliced
salt and freshly ground black pepper

Trim and wash the kale, then drain. Bring 1.5 litres/2½ pints salted water to the boil in a pan and add the potatoes, then reduce the heat to a simmer. Add the garlic and the olive oil. When the potatoes are cooked, remove from the pan with a slotted spoon, and liquidize to a smooth purée. Return to the water in the pan and bring to a simmer. Remove the stalks from the kale and finely shred the leaves, then add to the pot with the chorizo. Simmer for five minutes, adjust seasoning and serve.

CABBAGE VARIETIES

Autumn/winter varieties include: 'Winnigstadt', 'Holland Late Winter', 'January King' (white); 'Rookie', 'Ruby Ball' (red); 'Novusa', 'Wirosa', 'Wivoy', 'Ormskirk' (savoy) and miniature 'Minicole'. Spring varieties: 'April', 'Avon Crest', 'Spring Hero', 'Wintergreen' (greens). Summer varieties: 'Greyhound', 'Primo', 'Hispi', 'Duncan' (greens).

PURPLE SPROUTS 'Rubine'

BRUSSELS SPROUTS *Brassica oleracea* Gemmifera Group

Although traditionally cooked as a winter vegetable with roast meat, Brussels sprouts can be picked from late summer to early spring if appropriate varieties are grown; these may be sliced thinly and stir-fried. The plants are large and leafy, occupying a lot of space, and large quantities of sprouts are best bought from shops, reserving limited garden space for unusual types unavailable elsewhere. These include a deep red kind with a distinctive nutty flavour, and French gourmet varieties that produce small, delicately flavoured sprouts for tossing in butter or breadcrumbs, or serving with crispy bacon or chestnuts.

Modern F_1 hybrid varieties grow tall and slender, with numerous tight sprouts at the base of the leaves – reducing their spacing will encourage miniature sprouts, and plants can be arranged in a row, tied to a supporting wire like fruit cordons for a disciplined effect. Start plants in a back-up bed, then transplant to final positions in a sunny spot sheltered from strong winds; they like firm, moist soil, with a sprinkle of lime if acid.

Sow earliest kinds under glass in late winter, prick out 5cm (2in) apart in trays, and plant out 60cm (24in) apart six weeks later, after hardening off; for small sprouts, space 45–50cm (18–20in) apart. Sow other kinds outdoors in mid-spring, thin to 5–8cm (2–3in) apart, and transplant when they have 3–4 true leaves, using the same final spacings. Feed in late summer with general fertilizer, and support with canes. Water in dry weather and remove any yellowing leaves.

Snap off the sprouts, starting at the bottom of the stem, and use within 2–3 days; any surplus may be frozen. Sprouts improve in taste with an air frost or two on them – but let the frost thaw before picking as this can turn sprouts black.

KOHL RABI *Brassica oleracea* Gongylodes Group

This odd-looking brassica is grown for its round swollen base of the stem, which has a fresh, warm 'green' flavour. Most varieties have greenish-white skins but there is a hardy purple kind with beautiful leaves. The 'bulbs' can reach enormous size, but the best are young and no larger than tennis balls, at which stage the flesh is crisp, juicy and free from woody fibres. Peel bulbs thinly and finely slice for boiling or for frying as fritters. The leaves can be cooked as greens.

The best-quality crops are grown fast on light, rich soils (limed if acid), giving plenty of water when dry. To ensure their small size, space no more than 15cm (6in) apart – they can be used for edging beds or as a temporary catch crop between slower vegetables. Sow direct from early spring to late summer, thinning to 10–15cm (4–6in) apart, or start in a greenhouse and transplant. Pull for immediate use when large enough. Leave late crops in the ground, or dig and store the bulbs (with their central tuft of leaves only) in boxes of sand.

SPROUT VARIETIES

'Oliver' is the best sprout variety for late summer use, followed by 'Peer Gynt'. 'Rubine', dark greenish-red with a superior flavour, is ready in autumn; 'Noisette' is an old French variety with small, tight sprouts. For late crops, choose 'Wellington' or 'Rampart': both are tall, heavy-yielding and still firm and well-flavoured after freezing.

KOHL RABI VARIETIES

'Green Vienna' and 'Purple Vienna' are traditional kohl rabi varieties, the latter a good purple-skinned type. 'Lanro', 'Rowel' and 'Quickstar' are slow to turn woody, even when large.

ORIENTAL GREENS *Brassica* species

There are a number of Chinese and Japanese leaf vegetables that can be very productive in small gardens. Most are also shapely and colourful, and look good in a potager, as edging, or bedded out in contrasting groups in large containers. They can all be eaten raw, stir-fried, braised or in soups.

Oriental greens can be mixed together as oriental saladini for sowing outdoors or in pots, any time between spring and autumn, as cut-and-come-again crops; thin seedlings to 2.5cm (1in) apart and harvest with scissors when 8–10cm (3–5in) high. Each kind also merits growing on its own. Many traditional types only grow well after the longest day, once soils are warm, but newer varieties can be sown earlier. Sow *in situ* or transplant at the 3–4 leaf stage.

Mustard greens (Chinese mustard) *Brassica juncea*

The dark green or red glossy leaves with fringed or crinkled margins have a mild mustard flavour and make a peppery contribution to salads and cooked dishes; you can also salt and pickle the leaves. Sow from spring to autumn and start cutting 6–7 weeks later as seedling crops, or leave to mature, when the flavour becomes quite pungent. Try 'Red Giant', 'Southern Giant', 'Miike Giant' and 'Amsoi'; 'Green in the Snow' has finely cut leaves and is very hardy.

Pak choi (Bok choi) *Brassica rapa* Chinensis Group

Plants form small rosettes of spoon-shaped leaves, which are dark green, glossy and sometimes lightly savoyed. This part is used like spinach, while the broad white or green leaf stalks are chopped and boiled or fried as a separate vegetable; alternatively, steam the whole plant – stalks and leaves. Plants tolerate hot weather and can be ready in as little as five weeks. Sow in summer and cloche during winter to maintain quality. 'Joy Choi' is the most popular variety; 'Mei Quing Choi' and 'Canton Dwarf' are compact plants for containers.

Mizuna greens (Japanese greens) *Brassica rapa* var. *nipposinica*

This versatile and prettily dissected vegetable is usually cut while small for salads or later for stir-frying. Use as edging, as under-crops for taller plants and on their own in pots. Sow from early spring to late summer; cut seedlings after 4–5 weeks or harvest like loose-leaf lettuce after ten weeks. For large plants, allow 25cm (10in) each way. 'Mizuna' is the usual variety.

OTHER ORIENTAL GREENS

Two other popular oriental crops are: Shungiku (*Chrysanthemum coronarium*), also known as chopsuey greens or garland chrysanthemum, which has spicy leaves and yellow flowers that attract bees; and Mitsuba or Japanese parsley (*Cryptotaenia japonica*), an evergreen perennial for moist, shaded spots. Blanch the stems like celery or use the whole plant in soups and stews.

Chinese cabbage *Brassica rapa* var. *pekinensis*

There is a huge, diverse range of Chinese cabbages – some produce large round or cylindrical heads of tightly packed leaves, others have loose, crisp leaves, and there are flowering kinds too. Unlike Western cabbages, these have a delicate, almost fragile flavour easily spoiled by overcooking. Use raw, steam gently or stir-fry briefly. Most kinds mature between late summer and midwinter, but there is constant innovation in this fascinating group of vegetables. Sow from late spring to early autumn and transplant 38cm (15in) apart each way about six weeks later. 'Kasumi' and 'Tip Top' have large, barrel-shaped heads of sweet aromatic leaves; 'Wong Bok' is round, solid and deep green; 'Orange Queen' is a solid cylinder of yellow or soft orange leaves.

PAK CHOI

Spinach mustard (komatsuna) *Brassica rapa* Perviridis Group

This has mild leaves and stalks and can be harvested as a seedling crop three weeks after sowing, or 8–10 weeks for mature plants. Sow between mid-spring and early autumn, and allow 30cm (12in) between plants. Cloche for winter use.

'(Witloof) Zoom' can be forced without darkness; red 'Rossa di Treviso' and red/white/green 'Variegata di Castelfranco' are radicchios that may also be forced like witloof chicory. 'Rossa di Verona' is an extremely hardy radicchio. 'Pain de Sucre' and green/white 'Bianca di Milano' are the main sugarloaf types.

CHICORY *Cichorium intybus*

There are three main types of chicory. Witloof or Belgian chicory is a coarse, leafy plant in its first season, but forcing it in winter darkness transforms it into fat buds of tightly furled leaves, the familiar white 'chicons' with yellow tips and a stimulating bitter flavour. It is eaten raw in salads and may be braised to accompany cooked meats. The heads of radicchio (red chicory) are densely packed, with crunchy leaves, usually pink or wine-red, and white stems; they have a tangy, bitter taste. Sugarloaf chicory produces huge unblanched heads of crisp, sweet, furled leaves. All kinds prefer fertile, well-drained soil in full sun, but tolerate less than ideal conditions. They may be grown in rows in beds but the radicchios, neat and richly coloured, look good in potagers or massed on their own in large

CHICORY 'Rossa di Verona'

CHICORY 'Variegata di Castelfranco'

CHICORY 'Forellenfleck'

containers or window boxes. Sugarloaf varieties, larger and more cabbage-like in appearance, are best grown in beds or deep boxes. Sow witloof chicory among flowers: dig some for forcing and leave others to bloom in their second year, when the sky-blue flowers attract pollinating insects.

Sow **witloof** varieties direct a few weeks before the last frosts, and thin to 20–23cm (8–9in) apart. Water occasionally in dry weather, and feed with general fertilizer at midsummer. You can force plants outdoors if you cut down all foliage in early winter, then cover the dormant roots with a 20cm (8in) layer of straw or soil. Check for chicons from late winter. Alternatively dig up dormant roots and trim their tips to leave them 15–20cm (6–8in) long; pack roots in 23cm (9in) pots with their tops just buried, cover with another (inverted) pot and keep in a warm, dark place: check after about four weeks. Discard roots after forcing.

Sow **radicchio** from mid-spring to late summer, **sugarloaf** kinds after the longest day and thin or transplant 15cm (6in) apart. The latest sowings may be covered with cloches in autumn to prolong their use. Use crops immediately after harvest, although sugarloaf kinds will keep in a cool place for up to two weeks. Either cut heads when of usable size, or treat as a cut-and-come-again crop.

ENDIVE *Cichorium endivia*

This is an annual salad crop related to chicory, available as curly (frisée) and the hardier broad-leaf or Batavian endive (escarole). Plants produce rosettes of frizzy or broad puckered leaves, rather like lettuces but with a notably bitter taste: this can be reduced by covering the centres with inverted dinner plates or special caps to blanch the leaves for 10–14 days. Sow and grow endive in the same way as radicchio.

SEAKALE *Crambe maritima*

This perennial must be grown at home, in a special corner or deep container, if you want to taste its juicy forced shoots during their short spring season. Seakale has bold, crimped blue-green leaves and enormous seedheads 60cm (2ft) or more across. Only the young shoots are eaten, blanched to a creamy-white crispness; they may be served raw like celery, or steamed or poached like asparagus.

In spring buy thongs (root cuttings) to plant 45cm (18in) apart, or sow seed outdoors; thin to 15cm (6in) apart and transplant the strongest seedlings the next spring. Water freely in dry weather and feed in spring with seaweed-based fertilizer. Force when 2–3 years old by mulching with compost, then covering crowns with special pots or upturned buckets in late winter. Check two months later and harvest shoots when 15–20cm (6–8in) long; uncover plants in late spring and leave to grow normally. 'Lily White' is the usual variety.

ENDIVE VARIETIES

'Fine Maraichère' (for summer use), 'Wallonne' (winter) and 'Sally' are curly varieties; 'Golda' and 'Cornet de Bordeaux' are hardy broad-leaf endives.

CARDOON   *Cynara cardunculus*

This magnificent thistle-like plant closely resembles the globe artichoke, but with paler grey-green, jagged leaves. The flowers are similar too, but smaller and less fleshy. The inner leaf stalks and midribs make a good winter vegetable; they are blanched like celery for 6–8 weeks to keep them pale and tender.

The flavour of cardoons is a more delicate version of globe artichoke; the stalks are boiled and served with a béchamel or cheese sauce, or with a blend of garlic, butter and anchovies, as in *bagna cauda*. The perennial plants are usually grown as annuals, in full sun and, ideally, light, fertile soil. They are supreme container plants, adding flamboyance to a terrace display or flower border.

Sow in late spring in small pots, 2–3 seeds in each, and pull out weaker seedlings to leave the strongest. Plant 50–60cm (20–24in) apart in soil fortified with plenty of compost, or pot on into containers at least 38cm (15in) across. Water in dry weather and feed with general fertilizer 2–3 times to promote fast growth. In early autumn tie the leaves in a loose bundle around a central cane, and wrap in a 45cm (18in) high jacket of cardboard, brown paper, or newspaper enclosed in black plastic. Cut off flower stems to conserve the plant's energy.

After about eight weeks, start harvesting by unwrapping the plants and either digging them up or cutting them just above ground level – leave the crowns in the ground if you want young offsets to transplant the following spring. Remove outer leaves and all topgrowth, trim off the fibrous skin and use the blanched stalks immediately. Cardoons can be overwintered with a mulch of straw. Varieties are 'Cardoon' or the larger, more succulent 'Gigante di Romagna'.

ROCKET   *Eruca vesicaria* subsp. *sativa*

Rocket, also known as roquette or arugula, is popular in Mediterranean regions for its pungently spicy contribution to salads. Since it runs to seed quickly in hot weather, it is best sown little and often, in pots outdoors or on a cool sill, in window boxes, and used as a component of mixed salad leaves cut while small.

Sow where plants are to grow, from early spring to late summer, and as soon as harvesting starts sow the next batch. Most soils and positions are suitable, but choose a shaded spot for midsummer crops and keep watered in dry weather.

TAGLIATELLE WITH POTATOES, ARTICHOKES, ROCKET AND PARMESAN

When plants are 10cm (4in) high, start picking the leaves, a few at a time, or cut whole plants 2.5–5cm (1–2in) above soil level. Their taste becomes more pungent with age. If sown outdoors in late summer, rocket will survive early ground frosts or, if cloched, can continue until the coldest of air frosts.

FLORENCE FENNEL *Foeniculum vulgare* var. *dulce*
This delicious late-summer and autumn crop, sometimes known as *finocchio*, is strictly a cultivated form of the wild fennel, grown for its aromatic seed capsules. Florence fennel has anise-flavoured leaves, like the herb, but is grown for the fat

RAISING MIXED SALADS

The mixed salad leaves so popular in plastic bags in supermarkets are easily grown at home, either in containers or in the open ground. You can buy special mixtures or blend your own (see page 76). **1** Prick out when seedlings have two true leaves, spacing them 2.5–4cm (1–1½in) apart in trays; cover in cold weather for fast growth. **2** At this stage you can start picking leaves or cutting whole heads; surplus plants can be transplanted outdoors after hardening off. **3** Alternatively, sow direct in warm soil outdoors and thin seedlings carefully; gently firm retained seedlings, then water well.

swollen bulb at the base of the 45cm (18in) plants; this is white, crisp and the size of a large apple. Plants need a warm, sheltered site (cold draughts cause premature flowering), on light, fertile soils with regular lavish watering. They look decorative grouped in large deep pots and boxes, or in blocks in the open ground.

To discourage bolting, sow soon after the longest day, in the ground or in small pots, and thin or plant out 25–30cm (10–12in) apart. Never let plants go dry (mulching is a valuable aid), and feed 2–3 times with general fertilizer. You can earth up the swelling bulbs or pack straw round them for a whiter blanch. Start harvesting in early autumn and clear before serious frosts; bulbs keep fresh for 2–3 weeks in a plastic bag in the fridge. Pick leaves for flavouring at any time. 'Perfection', 'Cantino' and 'Zefa Tardo' are bolt-resistant: sow from early summer.

LETTUCE   *Lactuca sativa*

Lettuces as we know them are not found in the wild, but continuous cultivation since ancient Egyptian times has selected and perfected a whole race of varied types, and today lettuce is the world's most widely grown salad plant. A lettuce

1

2

3

that comes straight from the soil is infinitely better than one which has been around for an indeterminate length of time in the shops. No variety has a very strong flavour, and lettuce generally acts as an indispensable background to other salad ingredients. It is usually eaten raw, with or without a dressing, but the crisper, more substantial cos types can also be braised or turned into soup.

The most popular is the cabbage lettuce (known botanically as var. *capitata*), a category which includes soft butterheads, with their soft, limp leaves and little heart, firm-hearted crispheads and the paler 'iceberg' type with its dense, almost transparent heart. Cos or romaine lettuces (var. *romana*) have crunchy, upright leaves and usually firm pale hearts, although some older varieties need tying up to blanch their looser centres. Leaf lettuce (var. *crispa*) has no heart, but forms loose rosettes of deeply cut or frilled leaves that can be gathered a few at a time.

Lettuces are supreme foliage plants to combine with seasonal bedding flowers: grow them as decorative edging to beds and containers, as ground cover in parterres, and as catch crops between slower vegetables. They are all grown the same way, although timing can be critical with some types designed for cool, short days or, like icebergs, for the heat of high summer. All kinds enjoy full sun (partial shade in midsummer, when excessive heat will cause bolting and poor germination) and fast growth in light, fertile soil. Frequent and regular small sowings ensure continuity – as a rule of thumb, sow for succession as soon as the previous batch of seedlings has emerged.

Sow open-air crops from midwinter indoors in pots or trays, and from early spring outside, either *in situ* or in a nursery bed. Thin or transplant small varieties 15cm (6in) apart each way, up to 30cm (12in) for the largest. Winter varieties for cloches or cold frames are sown from early autumn to midwinter. Do not transplant too deeply – the lowest leaves should be just above the surface. In dry weather, water regularly but not lavishly (this can produce bitter leaves), and preferably in the morning to avoid the risk of mildew on damp leaves overnight.

As plants in a batch of hearted lettuce tend to mature simultaneously, start cutting as soon as they are usable – lift the whole plant, and discard the roots and tough outer leaves. Pick a few leaves at a time from leaf lettuce or cut complete heads, leaving 2.5–5cm (1–2in) stumps to resprout.

LETTUCE 'Besson'

LETTUCE VARIETIES

There is an exciting choice of lettuce varieties. Explore a few unfamiliar ones each season, starting with reliable kinds such as: *Butterhead*: 'All The Year Round', 'Tom Thumb', 'Rossa di Trento' (red). *Crisphead*: 'Webb's Wonder', 'Beatrice', 'Blush', 'Imperial Winter', 'Saladin', 'Windermere'. *Cos*: 'Little Gem' (diminutive, with nutty, primrose-yellow hearts), 'Lobjoit's Green', 'Rosalita' (red). *Leaf lettuce*: 'Salad Bowl', 'Red Salad Bowl', 'Novita' (for under glass), 'Cocarde' (oak-leaved).

Salad leaves (misticanza, saladini) are simply mixed lettuces, chicories and endives, sown at high density in blocks and cut with scissors when 8–10cm (3–4in) high. If short stumps are left, seedlings will sprout again several times. Broadcast the seeds over a small square or sow in parallel rows 8cm (3in) apart, and thin to 2.5cm (1in) apart. They can also be sown in a cold greenhouse bed in midwinter for an early spring harvest before the high temperatures of summer run them to seed. You can buy special mixtures of summer, winter and oriental varieties; 'Miscuglio' is a blend of chicories. Alternatively, you can blend together all the various salad seeds left over from the previous year to make your own individual cutting mixture.

ICE-PLANT *Mesembryanthemum crystallinum*

The sprawling oval leaves of ice-plant are thick and fleshy, and covered in small sparkling 'pimples'. The young leaves and growing tips are the parts used to add a fresh, mildly salty flavour to salads. It is a tender perennial plant, best raised annually for growing as a shade-tolerant edging to beds and containers. Sow seed eight weeks before the last frosts, harden off seedlings and plant outdoors, 30cm (12in) apart, in any ordinary soil. Harvest leaves regularly, starting while plants are still young.

CLAYTONIA *Montia perfoliata*

Claytonia (miner's lettuce or winter purslane) is a dainty annual that will grow almost anywhere, even under shady trees. It is a very hardy salad crop, available all year round with winter protection from hard frost and heavy rain. The leaves, stems and flowers are all used as a mildly flavoured, succulent salad ingredient that is very high in vitamin C. Plants grow fast, soon flowering and setting seed, so make several sowings for continuity. Start in early spring for summer use, sow in midsummer for autumn, and again in late summer for winter and spring crops under cloches or in a cold frame. Sow in any light soil or compost, and thin seedlings to 10cm (4in) apart. Harvest for immediate use when leaves are large enough to handle. Plants self-seed freely, and seedlings may be transplanted in spring or autumn.

ICE-PLANT

PURSLANE   *Portulaca oleracea*

France is the main producer and consumer of purslane, although the mildly peppery leaves are also popular in Indian and Middle Eastern dishes. This tender low-growing annual, with its juicy stems and rounded leaves, has sprawling growth and makes an appealing ground-cover plant for light soils in full sun. Grow in patches in wide shallow pans, in rows in salad beds, or as an edging to paths and larger containers.

Sow indoors about six weeks before the last frosts, harden off and plant seedlings out 15cm (6in) apart; or sow direct after the frosts and up to mid-summer, thinning seedlings to the same final spacings. Pick the young stems when they are large enough to handle, leaving on a few leaves at the base, and use immediately. Remove any flowerheads that appear. The plain green species is the most productive; the golden form, *P. oleracea* var. *aurea*, is less prolific but looks very handsome in the garden.

SORREL   *Rumex acetosa*

Sorrel's shiny lobed leaves have a piquant flavour with a strong hint of lemon. They add vitality to oily food, produce soups and sauces and make a classic partner to salmon. Sorrel may be used anywhere as a substitute for spinach. A mound-shaped herbaceous perennial, sorrel will grow in the same place for many years, or you can start it each spring as an annual. The highly ornamental French sorrel is a good subject for large terracotta pots.

Sow in any well-drained soil in spring or autumn, and plant out annual crops 20cm (8in) apart, up to 38–45cm (15–18in) for perennials. Keep potted plants moist and well fed; open-ground plants tolerate drier conditions and light shade. Pick the leaves in small quantities and use soon after harvest; always prepare sorrel with stainless-steel utensils as the plant acids oxidize iron, turning the leaves black and unpalatable. Renew an ageing specimen by cutting the crown into small segments with a sharp knife. Cover a plant or two with cloches or fleece to prolong cutting into winter, or dig up a few roots and transfer to a deep box or pot under glass. There are no special varieties of sorrel. French, round-leaved or buckler-leaved sorrel (*R. scutatus*) is less acid and may be used in larger quantities.

SPINACH *Spinacea oleracea*

True spinach, with its rich green arrowhead leaves, is one of the most nutritious vegetables, high in iron and other minerals, especially if harvested just minutes before use. The plants are ideal for shaded, well-watered containers and as a catch crop between other, slower-growing vegetables.

Sow little and often in moist, well-fed soil that is not too light, and thin seedlings to 15–20cm (6–8in) apart. Repeat every few weeks from early spring to midsummer, and change to a hardy variety in late summer. Water frequently in dry weather, and feed with general fertilizer after the first 2–3 cuts. Overwintered crops benefit from cloche or fleece protection. Cut or pull young leaves, a few from each plant, for adding raw to salads. Harvest larger leaves freely, but gather

SPINACH AND RICOTTA TART WITH TAPENADE

plenty as they shrink dramatically in cooking. A little cooked spinach goes a long way, though, in a soufflé or roulade. Use as little water as possible: wash and cook immediately, letting the leaves melt in their juices.

There are many varieties, often grouped into summer spinach, and the hardier prickly winter kind, though some varieties (like 'Medania') can be grown at almost any season. 'Sigmaleaf' and 'Splendour' are slow to bolt in summer, 'Fordane' and 'Medania' are resistant to mildew in autumn, and 'Virkade' is good for winter use.

Perpetual spinach (leaf beet, spinach beet) *Beta vulgaris* Cicla Group

The larger, fleshy leaves have a milder flavour. Plants yield heavily for up to a year from a mid-spring sowing; alternatively sow in late summer for heavier winter crops. Grow 23cm (9in) apart in the open ground or in large, deep containers. Harvest regularly, especially in spring before plants start to bolt.

New Zealand spinach *Tetragonia expansa*

New Zealand spinach revels in poor, dry ground and hot summers; its small leaves have a rich flavour and a vivid colour. The vigorous branching plants can spread to 1.2m (4ft) across; grow as ground cover under sweet corn and climbing beans, and gather whole branches for stripping indoors. Start the tender plants under glass six weeks before the last frosts, harden off and plant 60cm (2ft) apart.

CORN SALAD *Valerianella locusta*

Corn salad (lamb's lettuce, mâche) is a hardy annual with blunt, spoon-shaped, dark green leaves in low rosettes. It is a prized winter salad ingredient, whose mild, nutty flavour blends well with celery and complements walnuts and Roquefort cheese. Plants take up little space, and grow best in full sun in any soil. Grow in rows in a salad bed, as ground cover between beans, or broadcast in pots.

Crops are ready in about 12 weeks but re-sprout slowly after cutting, often bolting quickly to flower. Make several sowings for continuity: in early spring for summer use, in midsummer for autumn, and in late summer for winter crops. Sow direct and thin or transplant seedlings to 10cm (4in) apart. Harvest individual leaves or cut whole plant, leaving a 1cm (½in) stump. Sow 'large-leaved' or 'English' corn salad at any season; 'Verte de Cambrai' has smaller, darker leaves, and is best for late sowings, as is the mildly minty 'Vit'.

SPINACH AND RICOTTA TART WITH TAPENADE

Serves 4 as starter, 2 as main dish

for the tapenade:
4 anchovy fillets
115g/4oz black olives, stoned
1 tablespoon capers
1 garlic clove
2 tablespoons olive oil

for the tart:
225g/8oz puff pastry
350g/12oz fresh spinach, washed
175g/6oz ricotta (preferably buffalo)
25g/1oz pine nuts
15g/½oz raisins
salt, pepper and grated nutmeg
olive oil

Preheat oven to 200°C/400°F/Gas 8. Finely chop the anchovies, olives, capers and garlic and stir in the olive oil to make a paste. Roll out the pastry into two or four thin bases, and chill in refrigerator. Blanch spinach in boiling water, refresh in cold water and squeeze dry. Roughly chop the spinach and mix with ricotta, pine nuts and raisins; season. Place the pastry bases on a baking tray and spread the spinach mix between them, leaving a narrow margin around the edge. Drizzle olive oil over each tart and put into the oven. Cook for 15 minutes or until pastry is golden. Top with a spoon of tapenade.

PEAS AND BEANS

Although members of this group (legumes) are technically fruiting crops, they are normally kept separate in the vegetable garden because of their remarkable ability to create nitrogen in their roots. Leaving their roots in to rot at the end of the season after the topgrowth is cleared will add free fertility to your soil. Peas and beans are easy to grow and crop prolifically if kept watered during flowering. Pick their protein-rich pods regularly to prolong the harvest.

RUNNER BEANS *Phaseolus coccineus*

Runner beans, with their scarlet flowers, are a favourite summer and early autumn climbing crop. If gathered young before their edges develop fibrous strings and used immediately, they have a fresh, well-pronounced flavour. The pods are sliced, then steamed, stir-fried or boiled rapidly until *al dente*.

Although strictly perennial, with tuberous roots like slim dahlias, the plants are usually grown as half-hardy annuals. Climbing varieties are the most productive, and make eye-catching screens with vivid red, white or red/white bicoloured blooms. Train them on poles or netting on walls and fences, and on 2–4m (6–12ft) cane wigwams in beds or tubs, combined with clematis or sweet peas. They also look attractive grown up the stems of large, single-headed sunflowers. Dwarf varieties (and tall kinds pinched to keep short) grow well under cloches or in smaller containers, but need a straw or bark mulch to keep their pods clean.

Choose a sunny or lightly shaded spot and work in plenty of compost. Sow outdoors two weeks before the last frosts, or inside in small pots a month earlier for setting out after all danger of frost. Space plants 15–20cm (6–8in) apart, tall kinds at the base of netting or poles arranged in rows. Water freely in dry weather, especially once flowering starts, and mulch. Pinch out growing tips of tall kinds at the top of their canes, or at 38–45cm (15–18in) high if kept dwarf.

Pick the pods before their beans start to swell – they should snap cleanly and juicily. Use immediately or keep in plastic bags in the fridge for 2–3 days; preserve by salting in layers in dark jars, which gives better results than freezing.

RUNNER BEAN VARIETIES

New varieties, often smooth and stringless, appear annually: among the best are 'Red Knight', 'Enorma' and 'Achievement'. 'Kelvedon Marvel' is very early, 'Painted Lady' has conspicuous red and white blooms, and 'The Czar' is white-flowered (said to set better than red kinds), with white seeds that dry well, like butter (lima) beans. Both 'Pickwick' and 'Hammond's Dwarf Scarlet' are compact and bushy.

FRENCH BEAN 'Purple Queen'

The pea-bean (*Phaseolus vulgaris*) is a climber with pods used like French beans and beautiful mahogany/white bi-coloured seeds, almost round and dried for storing. The sprawling winged bean or asparagus pea (*Tetragonolobus purpureus*) bears crimson flowers and 2.5–4cm (1–1½in) winged pods, which are steamed and served with butter. Pick them as young as possible, otherwise they become tough. Despite their names, neither is a true pea.

FRENCH BEANS   *Phaseolus vulgaris*

Snap or kidney beans (green, purple or yellow) bear round or flat pods, prepared as for runner beans and eaten raw in salads. Filet (Kenyan or needle) beans have slim round pods 8–10cm (3–4in) long; flageolets are grown for their fresh tender beans, rather than pods, while haricots are shelled and dried to store for up to a year. There are special kinds for this, although most varieties can be left for drying.

TRIPOD WIRED AT TOP

TRIPOD

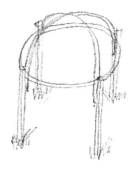

TIMBER AND METAL SUPPORT

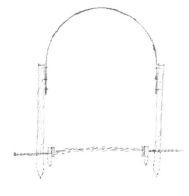

Though there are very productive tall ('pole') varieties, most French beans are dwarf, usually less than 45cm (18in) high. Treat all kinds in the same way as runner beans, but sow outdoors a week or two later as French varieties are more sensitive to cold; for early crops, sow in the greenhouse in spring and plant out under cloches 4–6 weeks later. Sow a dwarf kind again at midsummer to extend supplies into autumn. Prop up laden dwarf plants with twiggy sticks. Pick regularly, leaving none to mature, and salt or freeze any surplus pods.

Snap beans: 'Tendergreen', 'Sunray', 'Nassau', 'Royalty' (purple) 'Borlotto' (spotted and striped), 'Rocquencourt' (deep yellow). Filet: 'Fin de Bagnol' 'Triomphe de Farcy', 'Capitole'. Flageolet: 'Chevrier Vert'. Haricot: 'Brown Dutch', 'Masterpiece'. Pole beans: 'Climbing Blue Lake', 'Nectargold' (golden), 'Rob Splash'.

PEAS   *Pisum sativum*

Freshness is vital to preserve the tenderness and sweet flavour of peas, but since a 3m (10ft) row yields no more than 5kg (11lb), including pods, do not expect to harvest huge quantities from a small garden. A shrewder plan would be to grow choice or uncommon kinds – purple-podded, or snap peas for eating fresh from the plants – together with small sowings of green peas to pick young and eat raw in salads. Tall peas are the best choice for limited spaces as they give three times the yield of dwarf varieties; grow them on wide-mesh netting, strung on walls, wrapped around a wigwam of canes (see left) or trained up hazel sticks.

Perhaps the finest peas of all are *petit pois*, naturally small-seeded varieties that make an excellent dwarf hedge around a bed. Mangetout or sugar peas need no shelling; they include flat-podded varieties with the peas barely developed, and round-podded snap peas with fleshy, stringless pods. Shelling peas are either wrinkle-seeded – sown once the soil is warm – or round-seeded, which are hardier but starchy in texture. First early varieties, ready 11–12 weeks after sowing, are usually round-seeded; wrinkled second earlies (13–14 weeks) and maincrops (16 weeks) produce the sweetest peas.

Choose a sunny or lightly shaded site, on well-drained soil with plenty of added compost. Sow round peas in late autumn for overwintering outdoors, or in early spring; sow wrinkled varieties from early spring until early summer. Most mangetouts are very hardy and can be sown under either regime. Sow direct, 5cm (2in) deep and 5–8cm (2–3in) apart, in single rows or, for a hedge, in broad bands the width of a spade; sow in a circle around the outside of wigwams.

Water occasionally in dry weather until flowering starts, then soak plants thoroughly every week. Begin picking as soon as pods are well-filled, mangetouts when the peas inside are just visible, and check every 2–3 days: ungathered pods suppress further cropping. Surplus peas are best frozen. When plants are exhausted, cut them off at ground level and leave the nitrogen-rich roots to decay.

BROAD BEANS *Vicia faba*

This is one of the earliest new-season vegetables, especially if pods are gathered when 5–8cm (2–3in) long and cooked whole. There are two main kinds: hardy long-podded, sown in autumn, and short-podded varieties, reserved for spring sowing and considered the best-flavoured. If you pick and shell the plump beans while small, rapid boiling is all they need to capture their sweetness and flavour; they are a favourite ingredient of antipasti and other Italian dishes.

Tall varieties need shelter from the wind; they may be interplanted with peas, which use their stems for support. Dwarf kinds can be grown in large pots or window boxes, and make a neat, bushy edging for beds or larger tubs. The plants have handsome blue-green foliage and sweetly scented, lipped flowers, generally black and white although there is a fine crimson-flowered kind.

Sow hardy varieties in late autumn outdoors, others during spring, in rich, well-drained soil in an open sunny position or in small pots indoors. Set seeds 5cm (2in) deep, and thin or transplant seedlings 23cm (9in) apart each way. Keep moist, especially once flowering starts, and support plants with canes if needed. When the first pods form, pinch out the top 8–10cm (3–4in) of shoots to deter aphids – eat these tops as greens. Harvest the first pods when finger-length, the rest when the beans are no larger than hazelnuts. Both beans and pods freeze well, while large beans can be dried for stews.

Tall forms include 'Masterpiece Green Longpod', 'Green Windsor' (well-flavoured), 'The Sutton' (dwarf), 'Red Epicure' (red-seeded and, if steamed, retains some colour), 'Aquadulce Claudia' (very hardy) and 'Crimson-flowered'.

BROAD BEAN 'Express'

PEA VARIETIES AND SUPPORTS

Tall varieties, about 1.5m (5ft) high, include 'Alderman', 'Show Perfection' and 'Purple-Podded', all for shelling; 'Feltham First' is the best autumn-winter-sown variety. 'Carouby de Maussane' is a tall purple-flowered mangetout with flat pods. 'Kelvedon Wonder' and '(Hurst) Green Shaft' are sweet dwarf peas, 'Waverex' the best petit pois. Dwarf mangetouts include 'Oregon Sugar Pod' and 'Sugar Snap'. Climbing pea and bean varieties need tall, sturdy supports: turn them into flowering and fruiting structures such as arches, canopies, tripods and obelisks (see sketches opposite).

ROOTS AND BULBS

This group includes a number of important vegetables, among them potatoes, carrots and onions. They all share a liking for well-broken soil that is fertile but not too rich: overfeeding will dilute their flavour, encourage leaves at the expense of roots, and reduce the storage life of crops such as onions and shallots. Choose compact varieties for shallow soils and containers, and grow fast-maturing 'early' kinds, rather than the more bulky maincrops, in gardens where space is limited.

WHITE AND RED ONIONS 'White Prince' and 'Red Baron'

ONIONS *Allium* species

As the most used vegetables in the kitchen, onions could occupy a large space, so concentrate on growing less common kinds that are expensive to buy – red varieties, with their fresh, mild flavour, torpedo-shaped onions for slicing in rings, or sweet, white-skinned kinds. You can grow onions from seed or, more reliably, from sets – miniature bulbs with several weeks' growth behind them. They are planted in autumn, which makes good use of space over winter, or in spring for later ripening and longer storage. Grow them in beds, rows or blocks, although they also take kindly to grouping in tubs, boxes and other large containers.

Choose a sunny position in firm, well-drained, fertile soil. Sow overwintered varieties in late summer, maincrops in early spring, and thin to 5–10cm (2–4in) apart (wider spacing gives larger bulbs). Plant winter sets in early autumn, main-crops in mid-spring at the same distances, just burying the bulbs below the surface. Hand-weed carefully to avoid disturbing the shallow roots, and water in dry weather until yellow leaf tips indicate ripening.

Use split or flowering bulbs first. For storage, leave until the yellowing foliage collapses, then lift with a fork and dry in the sun or under glass. When skins are papery, plait in strings or store on shelves or in nets. Overwintered crops mature in early summer and keep until autumn; maincrops ripen in autumn and store until spring. Varieties include 'Red Baron', 'Red Epicure' 'Southport Red Globe'; white 'Albion' and 'White Prince'; torpedo-shaped 'Long Red Florence' and 'Owa'.

SHALLOTS *Allium cepa* Aggregatum Group

Shallots are like small red, yellow or brown onions (each kind with a subtly different taste), and produce a cluster of pear-shaped bulbs from each one planted. Less pungent than onions, they have an intense mellow flavour and are an indis-pensable ingredient of French cuisine. Site them like onions, or as edging plants. They were traditionally planted on the shortest day for harvesting in midsummer but modern, more productive kinds bolt if planted before early spring. Plant medium-size bulbs as for onion sets, but spaced 20–23cm (8–9in) apart, and grow, dry and store in the same way. Up-to-date varieties include yellow-skinned 'Atlantic' and 'Golden Gourmet', red 'Pikant' and 'Red Sun', and brown 'Santé'.

SAUTÉED ONIONS WITH GARLIC, ROSEMARY, OLIVES

This dish is excellent served with grilled rabbit or chicken. It can also be made with shallots. Serves 4

1kg/2lb small white-skinned onions
115g/4oz unsalted butter
2 medium-sized heads of garlic
salt and freshly ground black pepper
225g/8oz black olives, chopped
sprig of fresh rosemary, chopped
pinch of sugar
juice of a lemon

Peel and chop the onions. Melt the butter in a wide, heavy bottomed pan and tip in the onions, reducing the heat to a minimum. Allow them to sit in one layer only. Break apart the heads of garlic peeling each clove, and add them to the onions, along with the salt and pepper. Leave the pan on the heat for an hour or so. Check the onions every now and again, turning over occasionally, until they are quite soft and golden. Scatter over the olives and rosemary and mix in. Sprinkle in a pinch of sugar and, when it caramelizes, pour in the lemon juice.

BEETROOT 'Detroit Little Ball'

GARLIC VARIETIES

A garlic bulb is a cluster of pointed cloves, each of which will multiply into a complete new bulb when planted. 'White Pearl', 'Thermidrome' and 'Printanor' (planted in late winter) are all reliable varieties.

GARLIC   *Allium sativum*

Garlic needs exposure to cold weather, so plant in mid-autumn for harvest next summer. Its flavour, mild at first, becomes potent and lingering when dried, and provides essential flavouring in Mediterranean and Asian cuisines. Plant and grow like shallots (see page 85). Dig up plants when their leaf tips turn yellow, and finish ripening in sun or under glass before storing.

BEETROOT *Beta vulgaris* subsp. *vulgaris*

No other vegetable flaunts its colour as gloriously as a freshly cooked crimson beetroot. There are yellow and white varieties, with a sweet, mild taste, but they look pale and uninspiring compared with classic red kinds, best grown in the smaller garden as 'baby beet'. These take just 12 weeks from sowing to maturity. Beetroot's lustrous burgundy-red leaves contribute sumptuous colour to planting schemes – one variety, 'McGregor's Favourite', is recommended as a summer foliage plant for borders. The plants enjoy a sunny position in any fertile soil, and are good candidates for pots, tubs and window boxes, as well as decorative edging for beds and paths. Larger maincrops, taking up to 4–5 months to produce heavy roots for storing, are best grown in rows in vegetable beds.

Although traditionally cooked, beetroot are also good grated raw. The Russian soup *borscht* is the best-known dish, but there are other inventive ways to use beetroot, from roasting in halves with a coating of olive oil to slicing thinly and frying as 'crisps'. Cook the leaves like spinach or use when young in salads.

Beetroot seeds are capsules which produce several seedlings. Soak overnight to remove their germination-inhibitor, then sow where they are to grow, in rows or blocks; thin seedlings to 5–8cm (2–3in) apart for baby beet, 15cm (6in) for maincrops. Start with any small beet in early or mid-spring, and repeat at monthly intervals until midsummer, when maincrop types are sown. For very early crops, sow 4–5 weeks before the last frosts, using a bolt-resistant variety and sowing in modules, 2–3 seeds per cell; leave seedlings unthinned, and plant out after the frosts, spacing intact modules 20cm (8in) apart.

Water regularly in dry weather, and when roots start to swell feed with a high-potash fertilizer. Start pulling roots when 5cm (2in) across. Leave maincrops outdoors for use as required, or dig up in mid-autumn: twist off the foliage, leaving 2.5–5cm (1–2in) of stalks, and store in plastic bags in a frost-free place.

TURNIP *Brassica rapa* Rapifera Group

Like baby beet, small turnips are a favourite chef's crop that matures fast (6–8 weeks) and may be tucked in among other vegetables, especially if you find their plain foliage uninspiring. Larger roots, used in winter stews, demand a lot of

BEETROOT VARIETIES

Choose a bolt-resistant variety of beetroot for the earliest sowings (other kinds flower quickly if sown in cold soils): these include 'Boltardy', 'Avon Early', 'Bikores' and 'Moneta'. 'Golden' is a yellow-fleshed maincrop, 'Forono' large and shaped like a tankard, and 'Barbabietola di Chioggia' has red and white internal rings (pink after cooking).

TURNIP 'Snowball'

CARROTS IN OLIVE OIL, LEMON AND DILL

Serves 4

6–8 medium-sized carrots

1 onion

1 small stick of celery

140ml/5fl oz olive oil

salt and freshly ground black pepper

pinch of sugar

juice of a lemon

1 tablespoon fresh dill, chopped

Peel the carrots and slice diagonally. Fry the onion and celery gently in olive oil in a pan. When soft, add the carrot slices, salt, pepper and sugar. Stir well, then put a lid on the pan. Cook for 25 minutes until the carrots are tender. Add lemon juice and chopped dill and mix well. Serve at room temperature.

space and are unsuitable for small gardens, although some gardeners sow these very early while there is still spare ground, and crop the tops as greens.

Baby turnips have flat or rounded roots, usually all-white or with a reddish-purple top; they are mild, tender and juicy while young, with a delicious warm hint of radish, particularly when grated raw. They take kindly to any cool moist soil, even a shallow one, provided it is not acid (turnips are cabbage relatives), and they tolerate light shade in summer. Grow as a catch crop, in beds or wide shallow pots, and combine with beetroot for colour. Sow as for baby beet, continuing until late summer, and start thinning plants while still small to about 8cm (3in) apart. Pull when roots are 4–5cm (1–1½in) across, or use before they are tennis-ball size. Twist off the tops, which can be cooked as greens.

For small roots, choose 'Milan White Forcing', 'Purple Top Milan', 'Milan Red' or 'Early Snowball'. 'Tiny Pal' is the best late-summer/early-autumn variety.

CARROT *Daucus carota*

Next to lettuces and tomatoes, carrots are probably the best fresh vegetable for home cultivation. They are easy to grow in any bed or container, and their filigree foliage is as pleasing as an elegant fern. Slim finger or bunching carrots are the best kind for small gardens, available almost all year with successional sowing, and the sweetest when eaten raw or cooked fast to a melting tenderness.

The type to look for are short early varieties, pulled while still small, often only 8–10 weeks after sowing in warm soils. Out-of-season crops take a little longer, while maincrop varieties need 20–24 weeks to produce large roots for storing: these require more space, but their thinnings are a delicacy for using like early carrots. They also need deeper soils, and are less suitable for containers, whereas early, round-rooted carrots grow well in shallow soils, half-pots and even deep seed trays. Early varieties sown late in a cold frame or under cloches can be kept on the dry side once full size, and will store in the soil until needed – use this method to ensure winter supplies, still small and tender, but with a hint of the stronger maincrop flavour that suits casseroles and soups. For the rest of the year, pull small crisp carrots and eat them raw or boiled in their skins. Their unique sweetness also makes a distinctive contribution to fruit juices, puddings and cakes.

CARROT 'Primo'

Grow carrots in full sun, early and late sowings in a warm, sheltered place. For earliest crops, sow a round variety indoors in late winter, about six seeds per cell in modules, planting out the clusters, unthinned, in mid-spring, 20cm (8in) apart or tucked among other plants. Start main sowings in mid-spring outdoors (a month earlier in frames or under cloches), and repeat every 3–4 weeks until late summer, cloching the last sowings in autumn. Sow maincrops in late spring.

Thin in stages to 4–5cm (1½–2in) apart, maincrops 8cm (3in), and soak with water in which a garlic clove is crushed to disguise the carrot smell from root flies. Keep weed-free and moist in dry weather (irregular watering can cause split roots) – no feeding is needed during growth. Start pulling when the top of the root is finger-thickness, and use fresh. Late sowings are safe left in the ground, under cloches or a layer of straw in cold gardens. Treat maincrops the same way, or dig up mid-autumn for storing – twist off tops and pack in boxes in layers of sand.

CARROT ROOT FLY

The carrot root fly finds carrot crops irresistible, but it can be deceived if its targets are hidden among other plants, a sound reason to grow carrots as ornamentals. Try mixing equal amounts of spring onion, love-in-a-mist (*Nigella*) and carrot seeds, and sow in rows or patches in beds, window boxes or tubs under fruit trees. Or grow in raised beds, since root flies cruise near ground level. Keep carrots away from parsley and parsnips, other root-fly prey.

JERUSALEM ARTICHOKE

Fast early carrot varieties include 'Amsterdam Forcing', 'Nanco', 'Primo' and 'Minicor'. 'Rondel', 'Paris Market: Parmex' and 'Parabel' are all round-rooted. Medium-size varieties 'Flyaway' and 'Sytan' are partially resistant to the carrot root fly (see page 89).

JERUSALEM ARTICHOKE *Helianthus tuberosus*

Standard varieties of this sunflower relative can exceed 2–3m (6ft–10ft) high, and are difficult to place in small gardens. 'Dwarf Sunray', however, reaches only 1.5m (5ft), with cheerful yellow daisy-like flowers in autumn, and it makes an impressive stand at the back of beds or in a tub, especially if underplanted with squashes, New Zealand spinach or a similar ground-covering crop. A row of plants will provide welcome light shade in summer for leafy vegetables such as lettuce, spinach or cauliflowers. They may also be used to support tall sweet peas or as a seasonal windbreak in more exposed gardens.

Each plant can yield up to 1.5kg (3lb) of non-starchy tubers, at their best in winter and early spring. Their flavour is sweetish (the sugar is a form acceptable to diabetics), with a nutty earthiness. Thin-skinned and quick to discolour, they are prepared just before use, and can be roasted, baked, boiled or added to stews and soups. The tubers dry quickly in the open air, so lift only when needed or store in boxes of moist sand over winter.

Plants prefer a sunny site and tolerate most soils if well-drained. In early spring plant small tubers 15cm (6in) deep and 23–45cm (9–18in) apart – wider spacing will give heavier crops. Water regularly in dry weather, and stake the plants in exposed gardens. You can shorten tall varieties to 1.2m (4ft) high around midsummer to reduce their ultimate height. Cut down all growth when it has withered in autumn; surplus tubers can be left in the ground to grow the following season, but their size eventually dwindles and it is best to replant tubers every 2–3 years.

'Fuseau' has long, relatively smooth tubers; avoid 'common' or un-named supplies, which are knobbly and a fiddle to prepare. 'Dwarf Sunray' has rounded tubers and small, bright yellow 'sunflowers'; tall 'Garnet' has red-skinned tubers, those of 'Sugarball' are smooth and round.

CHINESE ARTICHOKE *Stachys affinis*

Chinese artichokes, also known as crosnes, are well suited to container cultivation because plants spread freely in open ground and their small white tubers are easily missed. These are quite distinctive, about 5cm (2in) long, tapered and knotted or ringed. They have a crunchy texture and a delicate nutty flavour, especially when eaten raw in salads; they are also good stir-fried, added to risottos after blanching, or pickled in vinegar.

Plants are hardy perennials, with rough, hairy leaves and, occasionally, purple flowers. Grow in 30cm (12in) pots, planting 3–4 tubers 8cm (3in) deep in each pot. Keep in full sun or light shade, and water regularly. After growth dies down in autumn, empty pots and harvest the tubers for immediate use; store the rest in their pots until needed.

PARSNIP *Pastinaca sativa*

Large, well-grown parsnips need a long growing season and plenty of room for their lush foliage. For containers and small gardens choose a less vigorous variety, or grow miniature parsnips, which are sown later and grown close together to produce tender slim 20cm (8in) roots after only 14 weeks.

Parsnips are at their best in late autumn and winter, after frost has enhanced their aromatic sweetness, traditionally used to flavour soups, puddings and pastries. They are delicious when roasted around a joint or baked with brown sugar, and make a classic country wine. Grow in rows or blocks in well-drained open ground, in large deep pots and boxes, and in raised beds, combined with radishes, which can be sown at the same time, within or between rows, and will mature before the parsnips need the space.

Always use new-season seeds as their storage life is short. Sow between mid-spring and midsummer (earlier sowings germinate very slowly); thin seedlings to 8–10cm (3–4in) apart. Keep well away from carrots, as both attract root fly, and use a canker-resistant variety in stony soil. Water regularly in dry weather, to avoid split roots. Harvest from early autumn, as soon as roots are usable – leave the rest undisturbed, covered with leaves or straw in very cold gardens. 'Arrow', 'Lancer', 'Avonresister' and 'White Gem' are good varieties for large or miniature roots.

RADISH *Raphanus sativus*

Radishes are one of the easiest crops to grow, and you can have them fresh almost all year round. Summer or salad kinds, with small red, white or bi-coloured roots, mature very fast – in warm weather in just 3–4 weeks – and special low-temperature (greenhouse) varieties extend the season into early winter under glass. Winter radishes (including the long white Japanese mooli) take 10–12 weeks to produce much larger roots for lifting and storing.

Summer varieties are used while still young, when the roots are crisp and juicy, with a gentle peppery warmth; they are eaten raw, on their own as an appetizer with bread, butter and salt, or sliced in salads. The milder round or long-rooted winter kinds can be sliced or grated as a garnish, cooked like turnips, curried or pickled. Radishes grow best in full sun (light shade in midsummer) and prefer light, moist soils, with good drainage for winter kinds. Since they are cabbage relatives, add lime to acid soils.

Radishes are not very decorative plants during growth, but summer kinds adapt well to pots, window boxes, and even deep seed trays, and make useful catch crops and 'markers' if sown among slow-germinating crops like parsnips and parsley. Allow a few plants to flower and set seed – eat the crunchy and succulent unripe pods, but leave some to produce seeds for next year.

POTATOES *Solanum tuberosum*

Harvesting potatoes is like digging for buried treasure, and loses none of its magic with repetition. Bury a single tuber in the ground or in a pot of compost, and it will grow and multiply into 1–2kg (2–5lb) of potatoes with a minimum of attention. There are three main groups. First earlies – ready to use after 14–15 weeks – produce tender 'new' potatoes, thin-skinned and sweetly flavoured, for immediate use. Some recent varieties, called extra earlies, mature in just 10 weeks and are ideal for growing out of season, or in buckets, tubs and containers.

Second earlies take 16–18 weeks and give slightly heavier crops of tubers that may be stored or left in the ground to become larger. Maincrops, which take 2–3 weeks longer, need more space but produce the heaviest yields. They are not a good choice for small plots but make excellent pioneer crops if you are starting

FRIED POTATOES WITH BACON

FRIED POTATOES WITH BACON

*With garlic, fine waxy potatoes and good
bacon, there is great joy in assembling
this excellent little sauté. Serves 4*

1kg/2lb poatoes, such as 'La Ratte',
    or 'Pink Fir Apple'
115g/4oz streaky bacon
4 garlic cloves, peeled, finely sliced
3 shallots, peeled, finely sliced
1 tablespoon goose fat
salt and freshly ground black pepper
½ teaspoon chopped fresh thyme
chopped parsley, to garnish

Peel and cook the potatoes, then allow
to cool and cut into slices approx
1cm/½in thick. De-rind the bacon and
carefully cut into small strips. In a wide,
heavy-bottomed frying pan, heat the
goose fat and layer in the potato slices.
When they start to brown, add the
bacon and fry for several minutes
before putting in the shallots and
garlic. Fry for a few more minutes until
the shallots start to soften. After a
couple of minutes, add some salt, a
good grinding of black pepper and the
chopped thyme, then toss all the
ingredients together. Tip in the parsley
and serve at once.

with a virgin or overgrown garden: simply clear the ground, add as much compost
or manure as you can, then plant the whole area with maincrop potatoes,
choosing a well-flavoured, waxy salad potato like 'La Ratte' or 'Pink Fir Apple'.
Cultivating and harvesting the crop will help prepare the site for your later plans.

POTATO 'Concorde'

In the small garden, first earlies are the type to grow – they occupy less space and for a shorter time than others, and their crops of small young tubers are always welcome. There are round, oval or kidney-shaped varieties, with white or yellow flesh and a floury or firm waxy texture, and each has a subtly different flavour and quality. Experiment to find the kind you like, trying one or two new types each season, including the classic 'heritage' varieties that are now being revived in increasing numbers.

First early potatoes often fit neatly into cropping plans. They are lifted when the plants flower, usually in early or midsummer, and this leaves the ground free for main summer crops, including vegetables that must wait until frosts are past. In sheltered spots or under glass, earlies can be planted in containers – 30–38cm (12–15in) wide and deep, or larger – about 4–6 weeks earlier than normal, and also in late summer for winter use. Potatoes are best grown on their own, as their bulky foliage does not combine well with other plants.

Buy certified seed tubers, and lay them in trays to sprout for six weeks before planting. Plant outdoors a month before the last frosts, burying tubers 10cm (4in) deep and 30cm (12in) apart; a 30cm (12in) pot will hold two tubers. When growth is 20–23cm (8–9in) high, mound soil around the plants halfway up their stems to keep surface tubers covered. Water containers when dry, outdoor crops every two weeks. When plants flower, scrape a little soil away to test the size of tubers, and lift with a fork when they are the size of pullet's eggs. Save a few tubers for replanting in late summer, and use the others as required.

'Swift' and 'Rocket' are extra early varieties for planting only 25cm (10in) apart; 'Swift' can also be left in the ground to form larger tubers which make excellent chips. First earlies noted for quality include 'Concorde', 'Aminca', 'Foremost', 'Accent' and 'Duke of York'. 'Belle de Fontenay', 'Roseval' and 'Charlotte' are tender waxy salad varieties with early-maturing crops. 'Pink Fir Apple' is a tasty salad maincropper for planting wherever there is space, while 'Picasso' is a modern maincrop that produces enormous tubers for baking. Classic varieties include: first earlies 'Red Duke of York' and 'Ballydoon'; second earlies 'Catriona'; violet-skinned 'Edzell Blue', and 'British Queen'; maincrops 'Arian Consul', 'Dunbar Standard' and vigorous, weed-suppressing 'Arran Victory'.

SALSIFY *Tragopogon porrifolius*

Sometimes fancifully known as the oyster plant, salsify has long, slender, creamy white roots which are harvested in autumn and winter. Black salsify or scorzonera (*Scorzonera hispanica*) is a dark-skinned relative with pure white flesh. Both have been popular in Mediterranean countries since the Middle Ages but are uncommon elsewhere – a sound reason for growing them in the chef's garden. Their roots have a mild, nutty flavour and are regarded as a delicacy for serving on their own, boiled or poached in their skins, then peeled before dressing with melted butter or a cream sauce.

Plants take up little space and are quite decorative: salsify has tufts of blue-green, grass-like leaves and produces handsome reddish-purple flowers in its second year, while scorzonera produces yellow daisies if left a second year to fatten its roots. They may be grown in deep pots and tubs, or in beds of well-broken soil, in either rows or in small groups – both blend happily as foliage plants among summer flowers.

Choose a sunny site that is not too rich or recently manured. Sow seeds in mid-spring where the plants are to grow, and thin seedlings to 10cm (4in) apart. Water regularly in dry weather. Start digging the largest plants from mid-autumn, leaving the rest in the ground until needed; use immediately, as the roots dry quickly. Unused plants can be earthed up in late winter to blanch their leaves for spring harvest as greens. Scorzonera will produce larger roots if left for a further season, or if sown in late summer for use 18 months later; the flower buds that form in the second year are delicious in omelettes.

'Sandwich Island' is the usual salsify, with long sweet roots; 'Habil', 'Russian Giant', 'Long Black' and 'Maxima' are all very similar scorzonera varieties.

SAGE

herbs and
edible flowers

The inspired use of one or several complementary herbs will transform a bland or familiar dish into something subtle and memorable. These aromatic plants enhance the unashamed pleasure of eating fresh, well-prepared food, but also contribute a variety of health-giving minerals and vitamins – most herbs, after all, are also tonic or medicinal plants. Growing your own herbs allows you to discover individual flavours and experiment with combinations.

Herbs generally need less space than other crops. Even a window box can accommodate enough for a *bouquet garni* or an omelette *fines herbes* and, since frequent picking helps to stimulate generous growth, there will always be a surplus for preserving by freezing or drying. Most herbs have ornamental foliage, often with pretty flowers that you can use for flavouring or in pot-pourri, or simply leave to attract bees and other pollinators. Many herbs have a seductive fragarance, released into the summer air by a brush of the hand, so grow them near paths and doorways, where they invite handling.

All these qualities, combined with the drought-tolerance and minimal demands of most herbs, makes them immensely valuable for the chef's garden.

NASTURTIUM 'Peach Melba'

PLANNING AND CHOOSING

The popularity of herbs is due to the fact that these culinary plants are easy to grow, crop prolifically in small spaces and, as the best chefs agree, taste their best when gathered fresh. The choice of herbs is enormous. It includes annual and biennial species, which must be sown each spring outdoors or under cover in pots for pricking out; they are usually grown in relatively large quantities. Perennial herbs last for several years before needing renewal; single specimens are generally sufficient, and can be bought as growing plants or, in many cases, raised from seed. Often evergreen, they can be important design elements in beds and containers.

Planning for herbs   It is not essential to create a dedicated herb garden. Annuals may be sown like vegetables, in the open ground in rows and blocks, or in containers. Perennials will often tuck among other shrubs, as edging or ground cover, or you can assemble them in a window box, sink or trough. Some plantings will be temporary – short-lived basil in its many forms, for example, or pot marigolds with their brilliant edible flowers – and these can be grouped together to add seasonal colour and interest to corners of the garden where people sit. Herbs in constant use, such as parsley and chives, should grow conveniently close to the kitchen, beside a path or in simple clay pots; these can be rotated in sequence, to rest some while others are in use. At the end of the season a few can be brought indoors for winter use. Growing herbs is compulsive, and collections soon expand. You might consider gathering them all together in a separate herb garden.

Herbs in containers   Herbs make excellent container plants that somehow manage to look more appealing than just a pot of herbs, and, as long as you provide adequate drainage material at the bottom, almost any container may be used. Small thymes, marjorams and prostrate mints can nestle artlessly together in a stone sink to make a perfect miniature garden. Leafy woodland herbs like angelica and lovage need constantly moist soil and thrive in glazed terracotta, which dries out slowly. The majority of popular herbs, however, enjoy the dry conditions of their native sun-baked hillsides, and for them there is no better material than unglazed porous clay. Square Versailles boxes and other large containers are associated with taller herbs, especially formal bay topiary or standard rosemary. Wire baskets, lined with moss or straw, can house a collection of essential culinary herbs, while galvanized metal containers and tins provide a good foil for evergreen species.

HERB GARDEN DESIGNS
A bed no larger than 3 x 1m (10 x 3ft) will accommodate a large number of herbs, perhaps formally organized within dwarf hyssop or rosemary hedges. Below is a modern formal design for a simple, self-contained bed, accessible from all sides and housing a generous selection of herbs, separated by buried tiles or treated timber gravel boards. Larger plans with a symmetrical pattern of beds divided by narrow brick, concrete or stone paths have a classical authenticity.

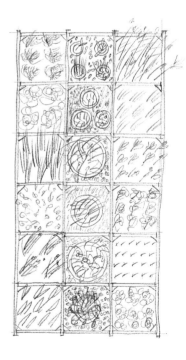

GROWING HERBS

Herb gardening needs no special skills. Annual and biennial species are sown every year, and the methods of sowing, pricking out and thinning are essentially the same as for vegetables (see pages 44–45). Perennial herbs need annual attention and occasional propagation to rejuvenate the plants and maintain good crops. All kinds of herbs benefit from the care taken over initial soil cultivation and drainage.

Soil preparation   Soft leafy herbs such as parsley and chervil need well-broken, moisture-retentive soil to sustain plenty of lush, fast growth, so break up the ground thoroughly with a fork and mix in as much well-rotted garden compost as possible before sowing or planting. Aromatic perennials like thyme, savory and grey-leaved herbs such as sage all require efficient drainage to prevent their suffering in cool, damp conditions – light soils will normally provide this, but heavier ground should be opened up by digging in plenty of grit or sharp sand. Fill containers with a gritty soil-based compost over a generous bottom layer of gravel or broken crocks for good drainage.

Planting   Before planting out herbs started indoors, harden them off to accustom them to open-air conditions. Most herbs are best planted in spring, which allows perennials time to settle in before the winter. Dampen pots and trays before planting, fork a light dressing of general fertilizer into the planting site, and make a hole just big enough to take the rootball comfortably – burying this too deeply can cause stems to rot. Firm in position, water thoroughly, then label them accurately. Mulch after planting, using compost for leafy herbs that enjoy moist conditions; grit or gravel for sun-loving species.

PROPAGATING HERBS

Perennial herbs, especially named varieties that cannot be raised from seed, are usually propagated by cuttings or division – this needs doing every few years to maintain vigour. Spring and early-summer cuttings use the soft growing tips (see opposite), rooted indoors in a propagator or in a pot covered with a plastic bag to keep them moist. Late-summer cuttings of tips and sideshoots can be rooted in a cold frame. Use a spade to divide clump-forming herbs in spring or autumn, replanting young outer segments and discarding the older central portion. The technique for propagating creeping herbs is described on page 109. **1** Trim soft cuttings to length with a sharp knife, cutting just below a leaf joint; remove lower leaves. **2** Insert in cuttings compost or a 50:50 mix of seed compost and grit or perlite. **3** Water to settle the compost; allow leaves to dry, then cover with a plastic bag until new growth appears.

Pruning and propagation   Regular picking is the best way to prune herbs; it encourages bushy, branching growth and prevents perennials from ageing and becoming woody or bare-stemmed. Most perennials benefit from an annual trim with shears or secateurs, usually just after flowering or in spring before growth resumes. The healthy trimmings can be used for propagation.

1

2

3

Harvesting   Pick foliage and growing tips frequently while they are young and well-flavoured, preferably on a warm, sunny day. As the season advances, leaves and stems become tougher, flowering is likely, and flavours change, but cutting back plants by half around midsummer or when flower stems appear can prolong their usefulness. Gather seed crops when nearly ripe, usually indicated by the seedheads changing colour, and harvest before the seeds fall out, enclosing complete heads in paper bags and suspending these in a warm place to finish drying.

PRESERVING HERBS

Drying and freezing (in plastic bags or ice-cube trays) are the main methods, although some herbs can be infused in bottles of oil or vinegar; flavours usually survive freezing better than drying. Gather leaves for preserving on a dry, sunny morning, ideally just before flowering. Discard preserved herbs when the new crop becomes available; store ripe dry seeds in airtight jars.

ANNUAL HERBS

Annual and biennial herbs need to be sown each year, often in large quantities according to the amounts used, and are best grown in rows or blocks like vegetables. Pick regularly as they soon flower and seed if left unused.

DILL   *Anethum graveolens*

Appetite and digestion are stimulated by the delicious, slightly aniseed taste of dill's thread-like leaves and its even more pungent seeds. A key ingredient of the Scandinavian gravadlax (marinated salmon), it enhances most other fish dishes and blends happily with broad beans, rice, lamb and pickles. The fragile plants need sun and shelter from wind, so grow in pots or as patches in a herb garden.

Sow seeds outdoors in mid-spring and again at monthly intervals until midsummer for fresh leaves; thin to clumps 20–23cm (8–9in) apart. Support with twigs and water regularly in dry weather as dill runs to seed quickly in heat. Pick leaves as needed; cut yellowing seedheads and suspend in paper bags in a warm place until dry. Rub out the seeds and store in airtight jars.

ANGELICA   *Angelica archangelica*

Although angelica is best known for its candied stems, the young leaves help reduce the acidity of cooked rhubarb or gooseberries and add a hint of muscatel. With midday shade and plenty of moisture, huge clumps of bright green leaves develop in the first year. The following year, stout branching stems, 1.8m (6ft) tall, bear broad, scented white flowerheads, after which the plant self-seeds and dies. Angelica looks magnificent in island beds or in deep containers of rich compost against a wall. Keep seeds in the refrigerator, then sow in autumn or mid-spring, thinning to 45cm (18in) apart. Water well in dry weather. Use young leaves fresh at any time; cut stems to candy in the second spring.

CHERVIL   *Anthriscus cerefolium*

This delicate fern-leaved *fine herbe* can be harvested fresh all year round just 6–8 weeks after sowing. Pick lavishly for flavouring vegetables, white fish, eggs

DILL

DILL VARIETIES

'Bouquet' and 'Fernleaf' are dwarf varieties, 'Vierling' the largest; 'Sari' and 'Dukat' are best for leaves; 'Mammoth' for seeds.

and salads with subtle hints of parsley and aniseed. The 30cm (12in) hardy annual plants prefer lightly shaded moist soil. Sow every few weeks from early spring until late summer, between other herbs and vegetables or in 13–15cm (5–6in) pots. Cloche late sowings or bring indoors over winter.

BORAGE *Borago officinalis*

This herb is grown for its intensely blue flowers, which are crystallized or sprinkled on salads, and its cucumber-flavoured young leaves, used in summer drinks such as Pimms and cold soups. The brittle, hairy 60cm (24in) plants are easily tumbled by wind, so grow among other flowers for support. Sow and grow as for pot marigold. Pick open flowers for immediate use or freezing; young leaves are best for fresh use. Plants will self-seed freely. 'Alba' is a white variety.

POT MARIGOLD *Calendula officinalis*

The vivid yellow or orange petals of marigolds are a valuable saffron substitute for colouring rice and decorating salads. They grow almost anywhere and make a cheerful edging or container subject. Plant next to herbs prone to aphids as they attract hoverfly, an aphid predator. Sow direct in spring and thin to 30cm (12in) apart; for early flowers, sow outdoors or in pots during autumn. Gather flowers when fully open and use the petals only. Deadhead regularly.

CORIANDER *Coriandrum sativum*

Coriander's pungent leaves are much used by 'fusion' chefs and in oriental food and are excellent in chutneys and curries. Their flavour is quite distinct from the aromatic warmth of the seeds, which are used in garam masala and toasted for fruit dishes and soups. The 90cm (3ft) plants grow fast in full sun with good drainage, in rows in the open ground or in large pots. Sow direct, in early spring for seed crops thinned to 10cm (4in) apart, and again monthly until midsummer for leaves – do not thin. Snip off leaves at any time and use fresh; cut whole seedheads when flowers fade, hang up in paper bags to dry and store the seeds in airtight containers. The same plant rarely produces good leaf and seed crops – grow 'Cilantro' or 'Leisure' for leaves; 'Moroccan' for seeds.

BORAGE

BREAST OF CHICKEN WITH BASIL, CHILLI AND LEMON

BASIL VARIETIES

BASIL VARIETIES

'Green Globe' and 'Green Ruffles'
(large, frilled leaves) are alternatives to
bush basil; 'Greek' has tiny pungent
leaves, 'Neapolitana' is large and
crinkled. 'Dark Opal', 'Rubin' and
'Purple Ruffles' are coloured forms, and
there are lemon-, lime-, cinnamon- and
anise-flavoured variants.

BASIL *Ocimum basilicum*

There are many wonderful varieties of basil with distinctive scents and flavours.
Small-leafed bush basil and the larger sweet kind are warm, slightly clove-scented
herbs, closely associated with Mediterranean food and tomatoes and the essential
ingredient of pesto. Plants are not hardy and in most gardens their season of
outdoor use coincides with that of tomatoes, but pots of basil crop until winter
on indoor windowsills. Larger pots 17–20cm (7–8in) across may be kept on a
sunny, sheltered patio. Forms such as purple-leaved basil look decorative in
window boxes. Sow indoors in warmth in early spring, and prick out into pots for
indoor use; sow outdoors after the frosts, in rows or in containers; thin to 30cm

(12in) apart. Pinch growing tips to encourage bushy growth and water carefully, before midday and not over foliage. Harvest young leaves regularly from the top to stimulate new shoots. Preserve surplus basil in jars of olive oil.

PARSLEY   *Petroselinum crispum*

One of the most useful and nutritious garnishing and flavouring herbs, parsley comes in plain-leaved and curly varieties. The former has the best flavour; do not use the latter as a garnish. Parsley is a good edging and container herb, growing lustily even in hanging baskets and windowsill pots. Sow in moist soil in early spring, and again in midsummer for winter use, thinning the slow-growing seedlings to 23cm (9in) apart. Gather whole leaves to use fresh, freezing the surplus in plastic bags or chopped in ice-cube trays. Leave a plant or two to flower for next year's seedlings. 'Bravour' and 'Curlina' are popular curled types, 'French' and 'Italian Giant' are plain-leaved.

SUMMER SAVORY   *Satureja hortensis*

This annual relative of winter savory is a renowned companion plant for beans because of its reputation for preventing flatulence. Its aromatic, thyme-scented leaves are also used fresh in stews and stuffings, and may be dried for winter use. Grow in full sun as an edging and among bean plants, where its pretty pale mauve flowers will attract pollinating insects. Surface-sow pinches of tiny seed in small pots in mid-spring and plant out 15cm (6in) apart after the frosts. Pick leaves and tips as required, and harvest for drying just before plants flower.

NASTURTIUM   *Tropaeolum majus*

All aerial parts of this versatile annual can be used: the peppery young leaves and scarlet, orange or yellow flowers are strewn over salads, the buds and green seeds pickled like capers. It is a vivid summer flower for any sunny, well-drained position; grow dwarf kinds as summer bedding and companion plants for vegetables susceptible to blackfly, climbing/trailing varieties on fences and among shrubs. Sow direct four weeks before the last frosts and thin to 10cm (4in) apart. Leave a few plants to self-seed. The mottle-leaved dwarf 'Alaska' is an especially good variety.

BREAST OF CHICKEN WITH BASIL, CHILLI AND LEMON

The clean, simple flavour of this dish is the clue to its elegance. Serves 4

4 large free-range chicken breasts, skin on
olive oil
2 fresh red chillies, finely chopped
juice of a lemon
salt and freshly ground black pepper
large handful of basil leaves

Season the chicken breasts well on both sides. Pour enough olive oil into a cast-iron frying pan to cover the base and heat it. Put in the breasts, skin side down, and let them cook slowly until a golden crust forms. Turn the breasts and finish cooking. Add the chillies, omitting some seeds if too hot, and roll the chicken around in the chilli-infused oil. Add the lemon juice and seasoning and stir again. Add more olive oil to the pan, heat through, then turn off the heat and let the chicken stand for ten minutes. Briefly return to the heat and, once hot, tear the basil leaves, add them to the pan and toss everything together before serving.

PERENNIAL HERBS

Perennial herbs increase steadily in size over successive seasons. Most are herbaceous, dying down in autumn, although some are deciduous shrubs with a permanent branch structure.

CHIVES *Allium schoenoprasum*

The mild, refined onion flavour of chives is best appreciated when the leaves are freshly snipped and added at the end of cooking, or sprinkled over egg, potato and cheese dishes. The dense clumps of fine grass-like foliage make a good edging to beds, window boxes and large containers.

Buy young clumps in pots for planting 15cm (6in) apart in spring, in sunny, fertile soil that does not dry out. You can also sow seeds direct outdoors after the frosts, or a month earlier in small pots. Water well in dry weather. Remove the flowers in early summer to boost leaf growth, or add to salads. Plants die down in winter, but clumps can be potted up in autumn for a windowsill indoors: water and feed regularly. Every 3–4 years, in spring or autumn, divide clumps with a sharp knife and replant.

TARRAGON *Artemisia dracunculus*

This tender species is French tarragon, with a stimulating taste somewhere between vanilla and aniseed. It makes a great companion to new potatoes, complements almost any egg, fish, salad and white meat recipe (especially chicken), and is an essential ingredient of sauce béarnaise. Vigorous, it spreads quickly by underground runners, so grow in a bottomless bucket sunk in the ground or in a pot at least 38cm (15in) wide and deep. Fill containers with free-draining soil-based compost, and position in full sun. Buy as young plants for setting out 60cm (2ft) apart in autumn or spring. Remove the flowers in summer. Protect with a mulch after growth dies down or move containers under cover. Renew after 3–4 years by soft tip cuttings taken under glass in summer, or by separating roots in late spring and replanting small groups in fresh soil. Pick sprigs any time for fresh use, and in midsummer for freezing.

TARRAGON

CHIVES VARIETIES

As well as the simple species, there is a fine-leaved form and an extra-large variety, 'Forescate'; white- and pink-flowered variants are sometimes available. Garlic or Chinese chives (*A. tuberosum*) are similar but with tall, flat leaves tasting of sweetish garlic, and bright, white starry flowers in late summer.

FENNEL *Foeniculum vulgare*

Garden fennel is a lofty herb, 1.8–2.1m (6–7ft) tall with soft filigree leaves, bright green or bronze in the cultivar 'Purpureum'. A single plant makes a dramatic sculptural impact, with plenty of leafy stalks for grilling with fish or lamb. Grow in well-drained sunny positions and small tubs. Buy young plants or sow direct after the frosts, thinning seedlings to 50–60cm (20–24in) apart. Water regularly in dry weather. Cut down topgrowth in autumn. Pick young leaves and shoots at any time; harvest ripe seeds just before they fall and store in airtight jars.

LOVAGE

LOVAGE *Levisticum officinale*

Rich moist soil is essential for this leafy, clump-forming perennial with a heavy celery-like flavour that is welcome in soups, stews and stocks. Plants can tower 1.8m (6ft) or more if allowed to flower, but the leaves then become tough and bitter, so remove flower stems unless the seeds are wanted as a celery-seed substitute. Grow in large, deep containers or a lightly shaded corner of a deep bed.

Buy young plants, or sow in a nursery bed in autumn or indoors in small pots in early spring, transplanting in early summer 60cm (2ft) apart. Lovage develops slowly, taking 3–4 years to reach full size. Water in dry weather and feed every spring as growth revives. Harvest the outer leaves as needed, just before flowering for freezing; cut seedheads as they turn brown, dry in paper bags and store in airtight jars.

LEMON BALM *Melissa officinalis*

The fresh, invigorating lemon scent of balm is popular with cooks and bees alike. The young leaves are only used fresh, to flavour vinegar, wine and summer drinks – handle gently to avoid bruising, and do not cook or use too lavishly as bitter undertones can appear. One plant will provide all you need, as the rootstock increases steadily and needs occasional division or annual chopping back. Plant in spring in any soil or a 30cm (12in) pot, green forms in full sun, golden varieties such as 'All Gold' or 'Aurea' in light shade; trim hard before flowering to maintain shape and good flavour.

MINT *Mentha* species

Mint comes in many species and varieties. Plain green **spearmint** (*M. spicata*), pungent **peppermint** (*M.* x *piperita*), and **apple mint** (*M. suaveolens*) with its rounded, woolly leaves, are essential for adding to new potatoes, peas, lamb and salads. There are many other mints, some like **ginger mint** (*M.* x *gracilis*) and **pineapple mint** (*M. suaveolens* 'Variegata') which are handsomely variegated, and others with lemon, eau-de-cologne or spicy flavours for cold drinks. All are rampantly invasive unless grown in containers, whether buried or above ground – the latter being preferable, as supplies can be prolonged by moving pots and tubs under cover in early autumn. All forms of mint like rich, moist soil, and full sun or very light shade.

Add plenty of well-rotted garden compost to the soil, and plant in spring. Shear plants hard just before flowering to encourage more young foliage. Feed each spring with high-potash fertilizer and, if possible, mulch with compost in autumn after cutting down the dead growth. Every 4–5 years, dig up the matted roots, divide and replant as small clusters. Roots may also be lifted in autumn for potting or burying in boxes indoors to force early supplies.

PROPAGATING MINT

Mint, tarragon, marjoram and other creeping herbs are all propagated in the same way, by dividing the matted roots into segments. You can do this in autumn or late winter, and replant the small portions immediately or pot up for indoor harvest out of season. **1** Use a spade to chop out small portions of

1

2

3

SWEET CICELY *Myrrhis odorata*

A few leaves of sweet cicely cooked with tart fruit can halve the amount of sugar needed, and years ago a plant was always grown near the door for this purpose. The soft, fern-like foliage grows in a mound, 60cm (2ft) high and wide, and smells faintly of aniseed when crushed. Add leaves to salads and omelettes, the crunchy, unripe seeds to ice-cream and fruit salads. Plants enjoy moist soil and light shade, ideally in a bed though their long tap roots tolerate containers at least 45cm (18in) deep. Sow outdoors in autumn and expose to frost, or plant in spring 60cm (2ft) apart. Water well in a dry summer. Pick fresh leaves and green seeds as needed.

the young outer roots of healthy plants. **2** Pull out any weeds and old roots, then trim each division to fit into a pot, pan or box. **3** Bed the roots in potting compost, at their original depth; water and keep in a bright, frost-free place. Plant out after frosts.

MARJORAM *Origanum* species

Sweet marjoram (*O. majorana*) is a tender perennial grown as an annual in cool gardens. Its neat 30cm (12in) bushes bear white flowers, attractive to bees in summer, and small, greyish-green leaves, highly aromatic, with a Mediterranean warmth that blends well with cooked meats and tomato dishes. **Pot marjoram** (*O. onites*) is slightly larger and hardier, with purple flowers and a more muted flavour. If it is grown in cool or shaded gardens **oregano** (*O. vulgare*) tastes very similar, but hot sunshine and dry weather concentrate a much headier spiciness, which adds a lively pungency to pizzas and tomato dishes.

They are all seductively beautiful plants, especially in containers. Grow in warm sunshine (gold variegated kinds in very light shade), in free-draining soil or compost, spaced 23–25cm (9–10in) apart, or closer as dense edging and miniature hedges. Sow species indoors in small pots in spring; buy varieties as plants for setting out after the frosts. Feed every spring with high-potash fertilizer, trim after flowering, and cut back by half in autumn; cover or house tender kinds to protect from frost. Divide and replant every 3–4 years. Pick leaves for fresh use, just before flowering for drying. Low 'Compactum', golden 'Aureum', miniature 'Nanum' and 'Gold Tip' are attractive oregano varieties.

GERANIUM   *Pelargonium* species

The many and diverse scented pelargoniums, usually grown as houseplants, are equally at home outdoors in summer in containers stood where they may be brushed in passing. Their perfumed leaves are used mainly in pot-pourris, but those of 'Lemon Fancy', 'Graveolens' ('Lady Plymouth'), apple-scented *P. odoratissimum* and 'Attar of Roses' can be added to sorbets, cakes and puddings if removed after cooking. They are all tender perennials for keeping outside only during frost-free months; bring old plants back indoors in autumn, or take softwood cuttings, as for ordinary zonal pelargoniums.

ROSE   *Rosa* species

Roses were traditional herb-garden shrubs, planted as hedging or for height. Fragrant varieties include the 'Apothecary's Rose' (*R. gallica* var. *officinalis*), 'Rosa Mundi' (*R. gallica* 'Versicolor') and the damask rose (*R. damascena*). Their richly coloured petals are used to make rosewater and to flavour syrup and candies. Plant strong-rooted bushes in autumn in a sunny position, in richly composted soil or deep tubs of soil-based compost. Feed in spring and summer with rose fertilizer, and prune every spring, removing damaged and old stems. Harvest petals when blooms are fully open.

SALAD BURNET   *Sanguisorba minor*

Burnet's tender greyish leaves are semi-evergreen in mild gardens, and add a refreshing cucumber flavour to green salads and cream cheeses. Grow plants as an edging to beds, and as ground cover under shrubs, in wild gardens and deep containers. Sow in autumn or spring in trays in a cold frame, prick out into small pots, and plant 20cm (8in) apart in dryish soil. Pick young leaves frequently to prevent flowering; plants set seed very easily.

PEPPERED LOIN OF LAMB WITH OREGANO

By almost charring the lamb on a fiery heat, the meat inside remains pink and succulent. Enlivening it with lemon juice and oregano makes this a great dish. Serves 4

900g–1kg/2–2lb 4oz loin of lamb
1 dessertspoon cracked white and
    black peppercorns
75ml/3fl oz olive oil
1 tablespoon sea salt
juice of a lemon
1 dessertspoon freshly picked oregano
    or marjoram, chopped

Trim any visible sinew from the lamb but leave the fat. Rub cracked peppercorns into the lamb and lubricate well with olive oil, preferably the night before. Crush sea salt into the lamb just before cooking. Heat a heavy-bottomed frying pan and put the lamb into it. Brown well on both sides, ensuring the pepper does not scorch. Once the meat is thoroughly browned and still yielding to the touch, remove from the pan, discarding any burnt peppercorns. Squeeze lemon juice over the lamb, add the herbs and leave to sit for 10–15 minutes before serving.

EVERGREEN HERBS

Evergreen herbs are some of the most useful plants in the garden. Many are colourful and shapely, meriting space in flower beds, borders and pots. They are especially good for siting in strategic positions, because they have a strong presence in winter when much of the garden might be bare.

LEMON VERBENA

LEMON VERBENA *Aloysia triphylla,* syn. *Lippia citriodora*
The fresh leaves of this South American perennial, evergreen above 4°C (40°F), have a strong, mouth-watering lemon flavour, retained for months after drying. Plants are tender and succeed outdoors only in warm, humid climates, so grow as a container plant, in sunny spots outside in summer, or indoors in a conservatory or cold greenhouse. Use as a flavouring for oils, vinegars, soft drinks, cakes and ice-cream; it can also perfume soaps.

Sow seeds in heat during spring and prick out into small pots, or buy plants and pot on gradually into 20–25cm (8–10in) containers. Outdoors, space bushes 90cm (3ft) apart against a warm wall. Prune to shape in spring and autumn, and feed with general fertilizer in spring; in winter keep plants almost dry. Propagate from soft tip cuttings in late spring or semi-hardwood cuttings in late summer.

HYSSOP *Hyssopus officinalis*
A very old medicinal herb with edible blue flowers in summer, hyssop is a good choice for containers and window boxes, and as a dwarf formal evergreen hedge around sunny beds. The shrubby plants are totally resilient, happy in a city atmosphere and undeterred by drought. Use the pungent minty flowers sparingly in salads, the young leaves with tomatoes, sausages and stews.

Sow in early spring indoors and prick out into small pots, or buy small plants and space them 30cm (12in) apart, or as close as 15cm (6in) for a dense hedge. Trim all plants after flowering, hedges regularly in spring and summer to maintain a height of about 20cm (8in). Propagate from soft tip cuttings early in the summer. Use fresh as needed, or dry in summer for a stronger flavour. As well as the blue species, f. *albus* has white flowers, while f. *roseus* is pink.

BAY *Laurus nobilis*
The tough evergreen leaves of the sweetly resinous bay tree aid digestion and stimulate appetite. Bay makes a fine topiary plant, often clipped as a mophead standard and grown in large boxes or deep pots. Frost can injure young plants, and even mature trees are shallow-rooted and may be harmed in severe winters – so site them in sunny positions protected from cold winds, and shelter or insulate containers in late autumn. Add the fresh or dried leaves to soups, stews and fish recipes, as well as rice dishes.

Plant in early autumn or spring in well-drained soil or compost. Water occasionally in dry weather until established, and feed containers every spring with general fertilizer. Prune to shape in summer. Pick leaves any time for fresh use, or for drying slowly in darkness. The green species is the most popular; golden 'Aurea' needs more protection from wind and frost.

'Miss Jessopp's Upright' makes good
topiary; 'Severn Sea' and semi-trailing
'Tuscan Blue' have rich blue flowers;
'Corsican Blue' is bushy and pungent.

ROSEMARY *Rosmarinus officinalis*

Sun-loving rosemary has a warm spicy, almost gingery flavour that blends well with lamb, baked fish, roast potatoes, casseroles and tomato dishes; it is good in bread, and may be tossed on barbecues and log fires to scent the air. It thrives on sunny walls, where it revels in the heat, and in large pots that can be brought under cover in cold districts.

Always grow in the warmest, driest positions, with good drainage and shelter from cold winds. Plant in spring, 90cm (3ft) apart – or half this for hedges; feed every spring with rose fertilizer. Trim in late spring and after flowering, and remove one or two old branches occasionally. Protect containers and less hardy species in winter. Pick sprigs of leaves any time.

'Icterina' has leaves in two shades of
green, while those of 'Tricolor' are
prettily splashed with pink and white;
'Purpurea' is deep purple. Pineapple
sage (*S. elegans* 'Scarlet Pineapple') is
tender, with pineapple-scented leaves
and scarlet flowers in winter.

SAGE *Salvia officinalis*

The lingering musky flavour of sage is indispensable in stuffings for rich fatty meats, and works well in mushroom, liver and especially veal dishes. It is often added to sausages as a preservative, and makes a classic tisane said to confer long life and vitality. Plain green broad- and narrow-leaved varieties are the kinds usually grown, but red and variegated sages are tasty and contribute rich colour to herb beds and containers. They are all sun-loving plants, their flavours enhanced in dry, well-drained positions, and they look superb in terracotta pots.

Plant in spring, 45cm (18in) apart; you can also raise species from seeds sown outdoors after the last frosts. Prune hard in spring, and root some prunings as soft tip cuttings; feed with rose fertilizer after pruning. Protect variegated kinds from frost, and move containers under shelter. Harvest fresh leaves at any time.

WINTER SAVORY *Satureja montana*

This hardy dwarf shrub tastes like a more peppery version of summer savory (see page 105) and has similar uses, but it is available all year round, especially if grown in containers that are protected from winter frosts. Plant in late spring, 30cm (12in) apart. Trim hard in late spring and again in summer if plants become straggly, and replace every 3–4 years with new plants raised from soft tip cuttings or by division in spring.

THYME

THYME VARIETIES

There are many varied members of the thyme family, some grown purely for their good looks or medicinal virtues, and a few so tiny you will find them sold as alpines rather than herbs. Two are outstanding for flavour: common thyme (*T. vulgaris*) and its associated varieties, with their pleasingly pungent warmth, and lemon thyme (*T.* x *citriodorus*), strongly citrus with aromatic undertones. 'Silver Posie' is a variegated, pink-flowered version of common thyme; 'Silver Lemon Queen' is a decorative form of lemon thyme.

THYME   *Thymus* species

Thymes are sun-loving herbs for dryish, well-drained conditions – moist, fertile soil dilutes the flavour. The neat, wiry shrubs are reliably evergreen and their leaves can be picked fresh all year round, common thyme for flavouring stews, roast lamb and chicken as well as stuffings, lemon thyme in fish or pork dishes.

Plant named varieties in spring, 20cm (8in) apart in dry beds, or in window boxes and half-pots. Species may be surface-sown indoors in early spring for pricking out into small pots. Trim hard after flowering, and also in spring if growth is vigorous. Renew from soft tip cuttings in early spring every 3–4 years.

WHITECURRANT

fruit

In terms of flavour and choice, fruit has suffered more from the needs of commercial production than any other type of produce. Countless classic, well-loved varieties have dropped from sight as growers are encouraged to concentrate on a few highly productive varieties that travel well and look irresistible on the shelves. Gardens have become sanctuaries for varieties renowned for their flavour, like 'Pitmaston Pineapple' russet apples, 'Cambridge Late Pine' strawberries and 'Laxton's Giant' blackcurrants.

Some fruits rarely make an appearance in the shops under any guise: you will search hard to find fresh red- and whitecurrants, alpine strawberries or blueberries, for example, because they are costly to pick commercially and rapidly lose quality on their way to market. By growing your own, you can help to prevent heritage varieties from disappearing altogether, and at the same time rediscover the flavour of summer.

Finding room for fruit in a small garden is easy. Most kinds can be trained in space-saving and decorative ways, which are often more productive, and many can be grown in containers, providing height and permanence among other seasonally changing crops.

APPLE 'Ellison's Orange'

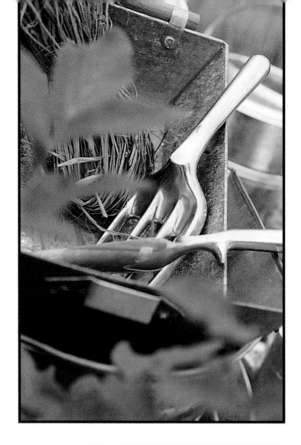

PLANNING AND CHOOSING

Fruit varieties differ widely in quality, yield and storage life. Home cultivation allows you to balance varieties that need immediate consumption with those that store well. When planning a collection of well-flavoured fruit plants, choose varieties that will spread the harvest over as many months as possible: a few of the earliest for eating from the tree and larger numbers of storing kinds to prolong the season into winter.

Avoid early-flowering and very late-ripening varieties in cold gardens, and select pest- or disease-resistant kinds for easy maintenance. Compact and upright varieties make best use of limited space. Remember that most districts have their own regional specialities which will grow well in your locality, and many old varieties offer special flavours and qualities worth exploring.

Good crops depend on efficient pollination at flowering time. Some self-fertile varieties are able to set fruit when grown on their own, while others (self-sterile) need to exchange pollen with a companion nearby, perhaps in a neighbour's garden, before they will fruit – identify these in a good catalogue.

A fruit plan Most fruit need light, shelter from frost and wind, and good drainage. Gooseberries and redcurrants tolerate a cool, shady aspect, but most others like as much sun as possible. Plants are bought either as bare-rooted specimens (these should be planted while dormant and leafless) or, more usually, in containers. Many fruit trees, at least in their early stages, need to be supported with stakes inserted before planting or on horizontal wires stretched between posts or on wall nails. You may have to protect ripening fruit from birds.

Fruit grow well in large containers such as tubs, troughs and half-barrels at least 38–45cm (15–18in) wide and deep. Use a rich soil-based compost with plenty of coarse drainage material at the base. Water and feed regularly, especially where cropping is heavy; repot or topdress in spring.

Siting fruit Make use of fences and walls for training fruit – there they take up the least room and benefit from shelter and reflected warmth. In the open ground gooseberries and redcurrants can be trained as small standards in a bed among other plants, and apples and pears as goblet-shaped trees which cast little shade. Training fruit simply involves cutting out unwanted branches and tying those you need to supports. The most common shapes include cordons, espaliers and fans (see page 121).

CONTROLLING TREE SIZE

For small gardens it is essential to buy fruit trees grafted on dwarfing rootstocks – the lower part of the stem that regulates growth rate – as these will limit both their size and vigour. Apple rootstocks are coded by letter and number: trees in containers and limited spaces are best grown on M27 rootstocks, where they will reach no more than 1.8m (6ft); otherwise choose the slightly more vigorous M26. Pears are usually grafted on to semi-dwarfing quince rootstocks. Apricot, peach and nectarine growth is limited by pruning, but there are also 'genetic dwarf' varieties which are miniature trees ideal for growing in large pots. Cherries and plums are unsuitable for small gardens and containers because a sufficiently dwarf rootstock is not yet widely available.

1

2

3

PRUNING FRUIT

1 With the exception of blackcurrants, whose older branches are removed wholesale, soft fruit bushes are pruned in summer by shortening new shoots to about three leaves. This helps to stimulate new fruit buds.

2 Similarly, trained tree fruit such as apples and pears are summer-pruned to check growth and encourage the next year's flowers.

3 Summer pruning and early training help produce sculptural shapes like stepover (single espalier) tree fruit: cut the main stem to about 40cm (17in), then train one branch on each side, supported by horizontal canes or wires.

GROWING FRUIT

Most fruit trees and bushes are long-lived perennials and occupy the same growing position for many years, so thorough preparation before planting is important. In particular, the soil needs careful cultivation, and trained plants must have adequate support. Once they have settled in comfortably, harvesting their crops is likely to be the most onerous seasonal task.

Soil preparation and planting Dig about a square metre of ground for each tree or bush, ideally two spades deep, and mix in plenty of well-rotted garden compost or decayed manure – if there is time, cultivate a month or two before planting to give the disturbed soil a chance to settle. Check that drainage is adequate and, just before planting, rake in some general fertilizer.

Water the plants in their containers (and the surrounding ground in dry weather) and allow to drain. Dig out a hole large enough to take the root-ball (or the fully extended roots of bare-rooted plants) comfortably and at the same depth as before, unless deeper planting is recommended. Make sure the knobbly joint on grafted trees is above the soil surface. Gradually refill with excavated soil, working or shaking some between the roots, and tread it down to firm a few times as you proceed. Secure the plant to its support, and finally level the surface. For container culture, follow the sequence for planting (see page 124).

Watering and feeding Thoroughly soak new plants whenever they are dry, especially during their first year. Check container fruit at least every other day in summer and while their crops are ripening. Feed open-ground plants each spring with general fertilizer, those in containers every 2–3 weeks between flowering and harvest. In spring, repot container fruits in fresh compost, or topdress larger containers by renewing the upper 5cm (2in) of compost. As competition from weeds can delay establishment, keep the ground clear around plants. Surround stems with straw or a porous woven planting mat; on dry soils, apply a mulch of organic material instead to help retain moisture.

Pruning fruit It is important to prune in the recommended season if plants are not to become too large and waste energy on unwanted growth. Using sharp tools, prune to a sloping cut just above a bud that is to produce new growth (see opposite page); clear away prunings, which might harbour disease. Secure stems with soft twine, and check all supports annually. Prune cordons, espaliers and stepovers in late summer, taking the new growth back to five leaves, then shorten these stems to two leaf buds the next winter.

TRAINED FORMS

There are three main ways of training fruit trees. *Cordons*: these space-saving forms are basically straight stems trained vertically or, more productively, at 45° (oblique); single, double and multiple cordons are all possible. *Espaliers:* these are upright cordons with horizontal branches growing to each side, usually in 3–4 tiers. Dwarf 'stepover' trees, ideal for edging, are freestanding single-tier espaliers only 38–45cm (15–18in) high. *Fans:* the branches are trained to radiate out like the ribs of a fan from a low main stem, supported by wires or a wall; they need plenty of room on each side.

OBLIQUE CORDON

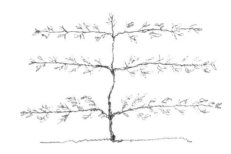

TRAINED ESPALIER

TREE FRUIT

Fruit trees provide the chef's garden with height and good structure. These permanent, woody plants increase in size over the seasons, although training and pruning will restrict their proportions. By combining dwarfing rootstocks with sensitive training, handsome trees can be tailored to fit a limited space.

QUINCE 'Vranja'

QUINCE *Cydonia oblonga*

You will rarely find golden aromatic quinces offered for sale. The low, freely branching trees have an attractive outline all year, making good specimens for the centre of a bed or a large container such as a deep tub. You can also train the slightly crooked branches on a warm wall, which improves yields in cold gardens. The apple- or pear-shaped fruits are acid and astringent on their own, but make a delicious jam or cheese; one or two slices add subtle fragrance to apple dishes.

Quinces are best grown in mild regions, in a sunny position on well-drained soil, with shelter from spring frosts. Plant while dormant and support with a stake or wall ties. Prune in winter, shortening stems to outward-facing buds and keeping the centre of the bush open, to produce a goblet shape or a fan on walls. Feed or mulch with compost each spring, and water well in dry weather. Gather the hard green fruits in mid-autumn, before any frosts, and store for 3–4 weeks until fragrant and well-coloured; they will turn yellow in storage. Isolate from other fruits to avoid cross-flavours. 'Meech's Prolific' crops while still young; 'Vranja' ('Bereczki') has very large, pear-shaped fruit.

FIG *Ficus carica*

In their Mediterranean home figs produce three crops a year, but only one in cooler gardens. Nonetheless, the handsome trees are productive when grown on a warm, sunny wall or in a conservatory. They have an air of distinction, with their glossy palmate foliage and long flexible branches which are easily trained; they will revive from below ground after savage frosts. Protect the tiny fruits formed in winter with straw or bracken. Gather the ripe figs when fully coloured, their skins on the point of splitting; they are best eaten the same day.

Plant in spring, in a large box or tub of soil-based compost, or within a buried compound of bricks or slabs to confine the wandering roots. Topdress with bone-meal every spring, then mulch with manure or compost. Water in dry weather, but not to excess or the ripening fruits will split. Prune out surplus and damaged stems in spring, together with one or two very old branches, and in summer pinch off the tips of sideshoots after 5–6 leaves. Check from late summer for ripe fruit. 'Brown Turkey' is hardy; 'White Marseilles' is a renowned, tender flavour variety.

SALAD OF FIGS, RICOTTA AND HONEY

Figs have an affinity with honey, and when cooked as here, with ricotta, they become wholly delicious. Serves 6

12 ripe figs
4 tablespoons of fine honey
50g/2oz flaked almonds
225g/8oz ricotta (preferably buffalo)

Preheat oven to 200°C/400°F/Gas 8. Make two incisions in each fig and gently peel back enough skin to allow the honey to be poured on. Place the figs on a baking tray and spoon a little honey over each one. Cook in the hot oven for 5–7 minutes, then allow to cool slightly. Scatter the almonds on another baking tray and cook until golden brown. Remove the figs to a plate and spoon over any juices that have collected. Crumble the ricotta over the figs and scatter the almonds around them, then serve.

1 Drill or hammer plenty of drainage holes in the base of the container. Part-fill with potting compost, over a generous base layer of coarse drainage material such as crocks or gravel. Use the tree to test for depth, and firm the compost before planting. **2** Remove the tree from the pot it came in and centre it in the large container; fill all round with compost. **3** Settle the compost in place, using your fingers; do not compact it. **4** Top up with compost to the depth at which the tree grew before and leave space for watering. Underplant the tree with small herbs.

1   2

KUMQUAT *Fortunella* species

Hardiest of the citrus family, kumquats have rich evergreen foliage and small, orange or golden aromatic fruits – these are a sweet-and-sour taste sensation, usually eaten whole or candied; they can also be preserved in brandy. In a large container, a kumquat is a designer's dream: leave it to make its own charmingly informal shrubby shape or prune it to achieve a gnarled, large-bonsai effect.

Plants need full sun and some heat, so grow them in containers that can be moved to a sheltered or frost-free position. Pot in a rich soil-based mixture, and topdress every spring with an organic mulch. Keep the compost moist but not waterlogged, and feed plants (ideally with citrus fertilizer) every 2–3 weeks from spring to autumn. Prune any time: remove dead or crossing branches and shorten others to required size and shape. 'Meiwa' and 'Nagami' are reliable varieties.

APPLE *Malus domestica*

With their wonderful shapes, attractive flowers and delicious fruits, apple trees are extremely useful for the small garden, where any tree must work hard to merit inclusion. Early varieties, ripe from late summer onwards, are eaten straight from

3   4

APPLE VARIETIES

There are literally thousands of fine apple varieties, and it is a good idea to try as many as you can at an autumn apple-tasting session before buying. Good dessert varieties include: 'Discovery', 'George Cave', 'James Grieve', 'Orleans Reinette', 'Ashmead's Kernel', 'Sunset' and 'Egremont Russet'. 'Rev. W. Wilks' is a useful cooker for small gardens. Cordons yield about 3kg (6–7lb) of fruit, while fans and espaliers yield about 10kg (22lb).

the tree, while later kinds can be picked in mid-autumn for storing in a frost-free place. A cooking apple is also worth considering but there are many dual-purpose varieties and any crisp, sharp eating apple is successful in salads and tarts.

Trained forms on dwarfing rootstocks are best for a small garden, where cordons, espaliers and fans make economic use of walls and fences. They can also be shaped to fit arches, screens or arbours where they are charming when covered with spring blossom, and can be productive from an early age. Choose a 'spur-bearing' variety rather than a 'tip-bearer', which fruits on long sideshoots and is not easily trained. Bushes and pyramid-trained apples are suitable for large containers or as a centrepiece in a bed. All apples need plenty of warm sunshine and shelter from spring frosts and cold winds.

Plant bare-rooted trees in winter, those in containers at any time. Support securely, especially in windy positions such as a rooftop. Water in dry weather, and feed in spring with general fertilizer or a mulch of compost or manure. Prune new sideshoots in late summer; remove the tips of main branches in winter until they reach the desired length; prune with the sideshoots thereafter. Test fruit for ripeness by lifting gently – the stalk should part cleanly from the branch.

APRICOT VARIETIES

'Alfred', orange with a pink flush, is early; 'Breda', dark orange with red dots, is mid-season; 'Moorpark', pale yellow with red markings, is fairly late. 'Pixy Hat' is another popular variety.

APRICOT *Prunus armeniaca*

Bought apricots, often hard and dry, are quite unlike their homegrown counterparts, which are juicy, melting and strongly fragrant, irresistible as fresh dessert fruit or poached in syrup; unripe apricots can be cooked, pickled or used to make jam.

Good drainage and plenty of water in summer are the secrets of success. Although the trees prefer fairly cold weather while dormant, their eye-catching early blossom needs warm shelter to set well – they thrive best fan-trained on a sunny wall or grown as bushes in large containers. In a conservatory crops can be lavish. All varieties are self-fertile, but a single plant under glass may need hand-pollination with a soft paintbrush if bees cannot reach the flowers. Buy trees on a dwarfing rootstock such as St Julien A.

Plant in late autumn or early spring, 3.5–5m (10–15ft) apart. The soil should be well-broken, with plenty of added compost and a little lime if acid. Water regularly in dry weather, copiously during summer, and feed or mulch in spring; dress with lime every 3–4 years. Fruits are borne on short spurs, so in summer pinch sideshoots to 8cm (3in) long to form spurs every 15cm (6in) along the branches; remove some old branches from mature trees to encourage younger growth. Thin clusters of cherry-size fruitlets during spring to leave single specimens; protect from birds. Apricots are ripe in mid- to late summer, when they are fully coloured and part easily from the spurs – pick carefully to avoid bruising. Use immediately or store for up to a week in the refrigerator.

PEACH AND NECTARINE *Prunus persica*

Peaches produce some of the loveliest blossom and luscious, richly flavoured fruits running with juice when ripe. Nectarines are similar, but with smooth thin skins and a livelier taste. These are supreme, if messy, dessert fruits, but may also be used in tarts and ice-cream. Picked when slightly immature, they continue to ripen at room temperature. They keep for only a few days; bottle any surplus.

Both peaches and the slightly less hardy nectarines grow well in gardens if their needs can be met. They like a brief chill in winter, with mild, frost-free springs and hot, dry weather in summer and early autumn; in cool climates they prefer warm, sheltered walls in full sun or protection under glass. Genetic dwarf

PEACH AND NECTARINE VARIETIES

'Duke of York', 'Rochester' and 'Bellgarde' are all outstanding peaches. 'Elruge', 'Humbolt' and 'Lord Napier' are good nectarine varieties. Genetic dwarfs include 'Bonanza' and 'Garden Lady' (peach) as well as 'Nectarella' (nectarine).

varieties grow to about 1.5m (5ft) high and wide, and these do well in large containers, which can be moved around to follow the sun.

Planting and cultivation are the same as for apples (see page 124). Water well in dry weather, and feed laden trees with high-potash fertilizer every fortnight. Cover plants in winter and early spring with a curtain of polythene or fleece to deter frost and prevent peach leaf curl. The early blossom on indoor plants may need pollination with a soft brush. Thin clusters of fruitlets in two stages until individual fruits are 15cm (6in) apart. Leave a strong sideshoot at the base of each branch in spring to replace the exhausted branch cut off after harvest; remove other sideshoots while small. Harvest fruits when soft at the base of the stalk.

P E A R   *Pyrus communis*

Pears are Mediterranean fruits, flowering earlier than apples, and preferring warmer summers and less rainfall to achieve top quality. In cooler gardens they can be trained as fans and espaliers on walls, where they are very decorative at flowering time. Most gardeners prefer to grow dessert varieties, to eat fresh or make into a classic dish such as pears *belle Hélène*, but there are a few firm and less aromatic cooking varieties that are excellent poached in syrup or red wine.

For small gardens, choose varieties grafted on Quince C, not a truly dwarfing rootstock but less vigorous than other kinds – you will still need to prune firmly to limit the size of open-ground and container plants. On house walls, annual training helps to restrict size while increasing potential yields. Pollination needs care: the popular 'Conference' is partly self-fertile, but others need cross-fertilizing with another variety from a compatible group – check catalogues before buying.

Planting and cultivation are as for apples (see page 125). Feed with general fertilizer in spring, and if possible mulch with well-rotted compost. Trees are pruned in summer like apples (about a fortnight earlier), although they make less vigorous growth and may need little attention in the early years apart from training the young stems of fans and espaliers. Pick fruits from early autumn, testing each by lifting and twisting it slightly – if it parts easily, it is ready. Store the hard fruits in a cool place, and check every week for first signs of softening, when batches can be brought indoors to finish ripening.

PEAR VARIETIES

The varieties 'Beth', 'Conference' and 'Concorde' all do well in cool gardens. 'Doyenné du Comice' and 'William's Bon Chrétien' have a superior flavour but need warm shelter. 'Seckle' and 'Winter Nelis' both have frost-tolerant blossom.

P E A R 'Fertility Improved'

SOFT FRUIT AND VINES

'Soft fruit' is the term used to describe the smaller shrubs and perennials that start early in life to produce their crops of soft juicy berries and currants. They occupy less room than tree fruits and yield heavily with very little attention. All will grow successfully in large pots, tubs and other roomy containers.

MELON   *Cucumis melo*

Ripe melon is wonderful in fruit salads, ice-cream and sorbets. Melons grow on hairy vines, trained on nets in a greenhouse or over the ground in cold frames in cool gardens; where summers are long and warm, they succeed outdoors on trellis against a wall or as a ground-cover crop.

Sow the large seeds on edge in individual small pots, six weeks before planting out, and germinate at 18°C (65°F). Pot on and plant out when 3–4 true leaves have formed, outdoors after the last frosts. Space plants 90cm (3ft) apart in rich, moisture-retentive soil, under glass in 38cm (15in) pots or growing bags. After 5–6 leaves, pinch out the growing tip and train the four strongest sideshoots on nets or evenly across the ground. Pollinate under glass by pushing a male flower into an open female bloom. Pinch out tips 2–3 leaves beyond swelling fruits; suspend in nets as they develop.

STRAWBERRY   *Fragaria x ananassa*

Sun-warmed strawberries selected for flavour and gathered fresh are an unrivalled treat. Most strawberries fruit for a few weeks in summer, and may be forced in pots or under cloches to advance their harvest by 3–4 weeks; perpetual kinds crop in late summer and early autumn if their early flowers are removed.

Buy certified virus-free plants in midsummer and plant 45cm (18in) apart in rich soil or compost. When flowers appear the following spring, feed with

STRAWBERRY GRANITA

*Piled high in a large glass served along
with a bowl of sun-warmed, just-picked
strawberries and a jug of cream, this is
one of life's great treats. Serves 6*

225g/8oz caster sugar
150ml/6fl oz water
juice of a lemon
900g/2lb perfectly ripe strawberries

Make a syrup from the water and
sugar, then add the lemon juice and
allow to cool. Hull and liquidize the
strawberries then pass through a sieve.
Mix the cooled syrup into the strawberry
purée and pour into a shallow tray;
place the tray in the freezer. As the
mixture freezes, stir with a fork
several times until it crystallizes.
Serve the granita in tall glasses that
have been chilled in the freezer.

STRAWBERRY GRANITA

REDCURRANT JELLY

Since desserts made with currants do not compare well to those made with berries, and as the jellies that currants render are of such excellent flavour, the jam pot is their natural setting. Redcurrant jelly has infinite uses, both savoury and sweet, from Cumberland sauce to glazing fruit tarts.

granulated sugar
freshly picked redcurrants, stripped from their stalks

Place equal weights of sugar and redcurrants in a preserving pan and warm over a low heat, stirring occasionally, until the sugar has dissolved. Turn the heat up and boil furiously for 10–12 minutes. Carefully pour into a jelly bag suspended over a bucket and allow to drip overnight; do not squeeze it. Pour into sterilized jars and seal in the usual way.

high-potash fertilizer and tuck straw or mats around plants to keep the fruit clean. Remove runners with their young plantlets unless you need them for new stock. Cut off all the leaves after harvest, and feed once more. Pick fruits, with a short length of stalk, when fully coloured. Use immediately after hulling. Small fruit from older plants makes the finest jam. Replace plants after 3–4 years with fresh stock or healthy young runners.

RHUBARB   *Rheum x cultorum*

This is the first fruit crop of the new season. Strong plants can be forced, producing even earlier crops of tender, juicy sticks with a delicate flavour. Rhubarb is naturally tart and is cooked with plenty of sugar. It is a popular filling for crumbles and pies, and makes a good jam flavoured with a little ginger. The thick roots

REDCURRANT JELLY

are unsuitable for growing in all but the largest containers. Light shade is acceptable; the earliest crops need plenty of shelter and warmth.

Dig the site well and add plenty of rotted compost before planting young crowns or divisions in late winter, 90cm (3ft) apart, covered with 5cm (2in) of soil. Feed in spring with general fertilizer and mulch with compost; water regularly in summer. Leave crowns undisturbed unless leaf stalks become thin, when you can dig up and split the crowns with a spade into small budded portions to replant.

Harvest lightly for the first two years, freely thereafter, by pulling sticks cleanly from the base. Crops are forced by covering a strong crown in midwinter with an upturned bucket or forcing pot, packed with straw; inspect growth from early spring. Do not pull stalks after midsummer but leave to grow unchecked. 'Champagne Early', 'Victoria' and 'Timperley Early' respond to forcing.

CURRANTS   *Ribes* species

Blackcurrants (*Ribes nigrum*) are high in vitamin C and with an indelible purple-black juice that gives an opulent colour to jams, ice-cream and cordials; combined with apples, they make fine tarts and puddings.

Red- and **whitecurrants** (*Ribes rubrum*) produce long strings of translucent fruits, which hang prettily on the bushes for weeks after ripening. Use redcurrants to make jelly; whitecurrants make classic small tartlets.

All three crops tolerate shade but fruit best in full sun. They need deep, fertile soil, but all do well in large pots. Red- and whitecurrants are upright and can be trained as cordons on wires; blackcurrants make large spreading bushes. Plant while dormant, 1.5m (5ft) apart, or 30cm (12in) for redcurrant cordons; bury blackcurrants 10cm (4in) deeper than before, then cut back to 8cm (3in) high to encourage new stems. Water well in dry weather, feed every spring with general fertilizer and mulch with compost. Prune blackcurrants by cutting out old, dark, fruited branches in autumn, leaving young pale stems. Red- and white currants have permanent branches with short fruiting spurs pruned in summer by shortening new growth to 2–3 leaves.

From midsummer pick whole strings of fully coloured fruit and rake off the currants with a table fork. Use within 1–2 days of harvest; freeze any surplus.

FRAMBOISE PARFAIT WITH FRESH RASPBERRIES

Serves 6

5 fresh free-range egg yolks
225g/8oz caster sugar
600ml/20fl oz double cream
100ml/4fl oz eau-de-vie de framboise
2 dessertspoons lemon juice
as many punnets of raspberries as
you like to eat

Place the egg yolks and sugar in a bowl and whisk at speed until they have trebled in volume and become pale. Whisk the cream until it has a soft, dropping consistency. Add the eau-de-vie and lemon juice to the egg yolk mixture, then fold in the whipped cream. Pour the mixture into a terrine dish and cover, then place in the freezer. Serve frozen, with raspberries.

RASPBERRY VARIETIES

'Glen Moy', 'Leo' and 'Malling Jewel' fruit in summer, 'Autumn Bliss' and 'Heritage' up to the frosts. Unusual kinds include 'Golden Everest' and 'Fallgold' (yellow), 'Glencoe' (purple) and 'Starlight' (black). Old varieties of raspberry, which are not disease-resistant, start to suffer after 8–10 years, so choose the newer aphid-resistant varieties above these.

GOOSEBERRY *Ribes uva-crispa*

Two generous harvests are usually possible from gooseberries. Berries generally set heavily and need thinning in late spring while still small – these are sour but, cooked with plenty of sugar, make delicious pies, crumbles and fools. Fruits left to ripen become large, juicy and tender. Red and golden varieties are often sweet enough to eat on their own; use green kinds for jam.

All gooseberries are happy in full sun or light shade, where they ripen a little later, and need moist soil in summer to swell the fruit and help deter mildew. Select plants growing on a short single stem or 'leg' to prevent suckers forming (multi-stemmed plants are hard to weed). Be prepared to net plants against birds.

Plant while dormant, placing bushes 1.5m (5ft) and single cordons 30cm (12in) apart. Water regularly in a dry summer, feed in late winter with high-potash fertilizer, and mulch with compost in spring. Prune bushes in winter by removing one or two very old branches, and any central or crossing stems that might hinder easy harvest. On trained plants, shorten new side-shoots to three leaves in summer. Cover with netting or sacking in spring to protect flowers from frost. Start thinning in late spring, picking alternate berries and reducing clusters to single fruits – leave the rest until fully coloured and soft.

RASPBERRY *Rubus idaeus*

Although their height makes them a challenging fit where space is limited, raspberries are wonderful summer fruits worth a place in any chef's garden. They can be grown in a single row as a seasonal screen or arranged round a central post to make a fruiting column. Four or five crowns will grow well in a half-barrel. Maincrop kinds fruit heavily in midsummer, just after strawberries, while autumn varieties, which are full of flavour, crop from late summer until the frosts. There are red, black, purple and golden raspberries, each subtly different and delicious.

The simplest and most satisfying way to eat raspberries is on their own, lavishly coated with sugar and cream, but they have an intense, tangy flavour that goes a long way combined with other fruits such as redcurrants. Use in tarts, summer pudding, pies and jams, or purée to make syrups and vinegars as well as to flavour ice-cream and yogurt. Raspberries freeze very successfully.

GOOSEBERRY 'Leveller'

GOOSEBERRY VARIETIES

Choose varieties carefully as there
are distinct differences in flavour;
in addition, some kinds have very
hairy fruits, and a few are almost
thornless or mildew-resistant.
'Careless' is a popular green variety
with heavy yields; greenish-yellow
'Leveller' has superior dessert flavour;
'Whinham's Industry' is a choice red.
For mildew-resistance, choose green
'Invicta' or red 'Pax' (also virtually
thornless). Hundreds of classic varieties
also merit growing: try 'Broom Girl',
'Golden Drop', 'Langley Gage' and
'Whitesmith' for fine flavour.

Add plenty of rotted compost before planting in autumn or early winter, 38cm
(15in) apart; cut back to 15–20cm (6–8in) high after planting. Tie in the new canes
as they develop, spacing them out along horizontal wires between posts or on a
wall or fence. Feed in spring with general fertilizer, and water regularly in dry
weather. Immediately after harvesting summer raspberries, cut out fruited canes
and tie in new ones as replacements; prune autumn varieties to the ground in late
winter. Check ripening fruit daily, and pick when fully coloured and soft.

BLUEBERRY COMPOTE

This gorgeous berry has a wonderful affinity with vanilla, giving the compote a memorable flavour. Serves 8

1kg/2lb blueberries
2 vanilla pods, split
225g/8oz caster sugar
juice of half a lemon

Pick over the blueberries and put them in a pan along with the two vanilla pods, the sugar and lemon juice. Bring to the boil, then simmer for 8–10 minutes, until the liquid turns syrupy. Allow to cool. Let the compote sit for a few days before serving with vanilla ice-cream and madeleines.

BLUEBERRY *Vaccinium* species

Highbush blueberries are large, leafy shrubs, 90cm–1.8m (3–6ft) high; you usually need two varieties to ensure a good crop. Each bush can produce 3kg (6½lb) of large, blue-black berries with a silvery bloom, and in autumn the foliage turns incendiary shades of orange and scarlet. The very acid soil they need is easily supplied if you grow them in large pots or tubs. With their rich, slightly tart flavour, blueberries can be used for sweet or savoury dishes. They are at their best when cooked and turned into jams and jellies, or added to pies and tarts; blueberry muffins and blueberry wine are classics. The berries ripen over a long period from late summer onwards and need successional picking. They freeze well.

Plants grow in sun or light shade with shelter from strong winds, in moist but well-drained acid soil; fill containers with ericaceous (lime-free) compost, and water with rainwater. Plant in winter while dormant, 1.2–1.5m (4–5ft) apart,

BLUEBERRY COMPOTE

water in dry summers and feed each spring with rhododendron fertilizer. Thin some old, dark wood from mature plants in winter, and clip to shape in spring. Start picking berries when fully coloured, slightly soft and covered in the bright bloom – use immediately or store for up to a week in the refrigerator. 'Bluecrop', 'Coville' and 'Ivanhoe' are all dependable; 'Herbert' has outstanding flavour.

GRAPE *Vitis vinifera*

Biblical tradition asserted that every gardener has the right to sit under his own fig tree and grapevine. The latter is certain to flourish, even in cold gardens, and makes an attractive trained climber over a seat, archway or pergola, but fruiting depends on climate and variety. The hardiest grapes are wine varieties, and only a few dessert kinds succeed outdoors, in warm gardens or protected on sunny walls. Under glass, however, many varieties produce fine dessert grapes without extra heating. The best flavoured grapes are served on their own for dessert, laid on a bed of vine leaves, but most kinds are also used in fish or game dishes, either as they are or after scalding and peeling. They may be added to salads and used to make jellies and juice. Vine leaves are used in Middle Eastern recipes.

Grapevines need well-drained fertile soil or gritty soil-based compost if grown in containers or a conservatory border. Plant in winter, no closer than 1.2m (4ft) apart, and against a south, south-west or south-east-facing wall if possible; tie stems to vertical supports or horizontal wires as they grow. Feed in spring with general fertilizer or mulch with compost; water and feed containers regularly.

Shorten outdoor vines growing over a wall or structure by one-third each winter until they have made enough coverage. On wires and under glass train a single shoot vertically; fruiting sideshoots form on each side and these should be cut back after leaf-fall to two buds. During the winter months, remove all loose bark on indoor vines to expose red spider mite and mealy bug. Spray or paint with tar-based winter wash. When indoor grapes flower, pollinate by tapping branches sharply with a cane or dab the flowers with a paintbrush or cotton wool. Limit bunches to one per sideshoot, or 30cm (12in) apart along branches. Use narrow scissors to thin grapes while small, cutting out overcrowded inner berries. Test for ripeness when fully coloured and in bloom.

GRAPE

GRAPE VARIETIES

Sweetwater grapes have large, sweet, juicy berries; muscats are perfumed and need heat to ripen. There are red, white and black varieties in each group. Fine indoor varieties include 'Foster's Seedling', 'Black Hamburg', 'Royal Muscadine' and 'Muscat of Alexandria'. Outdoors try 'Concord' or 'New York Muscat' for dessert; 'Siegerrebe' and 'Tereshkova' for wine or dessert.

PLANT CARE

If you follow these simple guidelines to the establishment and routine care of your food crops, whether they are growing in the open ground or in containers, you should encounter few problems between sowing the seeds and harvesting your produce. Careful soil preparation and regular watering and feeding will help to produce strong, vigorous plants that are less susceptible to pests and diseases – and that are full of flavour. A kitchen garden is not low in maintenance, but tending a small plot or a collection of containers should take only a couple of hours a week, and is all part of the enjoyment of growing your own.

Soil improvement If an established garden is full of healthy plants, there is probably little wrong with the soil, and any necessary improvement will follow from routine cultivation. Where its quality is unknown, however, you should buy a basic soil testing kit and carry out a few simple checks to discover if it is acid or alkaline – most food crops like neutral or slightly acid soil, but the cabbage family needs alkaline conditions, which can be supplied by adding lime to the soil at planting time. Any deficiencies in major nutrients may also be revealed.

Careful examination can tell you a lot about your soil. If it lies wet after rain, perhaps with puddles on the surface, it is probably heavy, with a high clay content and poor drainage. These soils stay cold for a long time in spring and may be prone to waterlogging, but if broken up by digging they can be naturally very fertile. The addition of grit when digging is also beneficial. Fast drying to a powdery consistency after rainfall indicates a light, sandy soil that warms up quickly in spring and is easily cultivated, but it might be hungry (rainfall soon washes out nutrients) and could need lavish watering in dry weather. Confirm your tests by rolling a handful of soil into a ball: a light soil will disintegrate straight away, whereas clay soil can be moulded, even polished to a shine with your thumb.

To a certain extent you have to accept the character of the soil: none is perfect, but all can be improved. Digging the ground thoroughly and working in plenty of compost or well-rotted manure will add body and substance to light soils and break up heavier kinds to improve their drainage and aeration. Regular mulching protects the surface from both heavy rain and hot sunshine, so preserving its cool, crumbly texture, and routine cultivation will keep it open and fertile. In difficult cases you might have to adopt alternative measures for the first few years while the fertility of the soil builds up: concentrate on small plants (especially root crops) if the soil is shallow, for example, but do not grow carrots, parsnips and other long-rooted crops on stony soil, or they will tend to fork when they hit the stones.

Use containers or raised beds to create special environments for fussy plants. On very thin, light soils grow greens and leaf crops instead of hearted cabbages.

Watering and feeding Consistently moist soil supports the fastest growth. Check containers regularly, daily in hot weather. Crops grown on open ground survive longer before wilting, especially if mulched or grown in soil with plenty of compost (see below). Aim to soak rather than dampen plants with a sprinkle of water (collected rainwater is best). As a rough guide light soils need watering weekly in dry weather, heavier soils every 10–14 days. Always use a rose or spray on cans and hosepipes to avoid compacting or washing away the soil.

As a general rule, add a 5cm (2in) layer of garden compost or a dressing of fertilizer to the soil before sowing or planting each crop – this will usually supply enough food throughout its life. Some crops benefit from additional feeding during growth, and this is stated in the individual entries - use a general or balanced feed, such as tomato fertilizer, unless another type is specified. Feed container-grown crops every week, starting about six weeks after planting in fresh compost.

Making compost for fertility   Food crops quickly exhaust fertility unless you return at least as much as they take from the soil. Making your own compost is a productive way to recycle garden and kitchen waste, and, if supplemented with small amounts of fertilizer, will restore depleted nutrients for subsequent crops. Anything that was once growing can be turned into compost, although it is best to avoid perennial weeds and seeding or diseased plants. To keep soil fertility topped up, simply add well-rotted compost wherever you sow or plant a crop. It is also easy to make your own leafmould to dig into the garden or use as a mulch.

Heat is essential for fast, efficient decomposition, and garden compost is best made in an enclosed container to minimize heat loss as the contents rot down. Square timber boxes – in pairs, so that you are filling one while the other decays – are visually satisfying and take up little room; brick, breeze block and plastic containers can also be used, and even redundant beehives have found new life as compost bins.

Harvesting   Gather crops regularly, starting while they are young. This encourages further yields and ensures quality – peas, for example, stop flowering if pods are left on, while beans become tough and fibrous and courgette plants will not flourish unless the fruits are picked regularly when small. Harvest most crops, especially soft fruit, for immediate use while in peak condition, clearing the last pickings for storing or preserving before they age. One exception is rocket, which can improve in taste if left until it is older.

Managing containers   When potting up food plants, start with a layer of drainage material in the bottom of the container – broken crocks and pebbles are suitable – and fill with an appropriate good-quality compost (see page 27). Position plants at the same depth as they grew before, and keep the surface of the compost level below the pot rim, leaving room to water. Stand large containers on pieces of tile so that surplus water can escape quickly.

All containers need regular watering, but small ones need it more often, especially if they are in full sun or exposed to wind. If possible, water pots in the evening to minimize moisture loss through evaporation, and always fill them to the brim or stand them in saucers of water until no more is absorbed. Perennial plants such as artichokes or herbaceous herbs in large containers will need repotting in fresh compost each spring, in the same pot or one size larger if they are still developing. Older plants only need 'topdressing' by replacing the top 5cm (2in) of compost with a fresh supply.

In winter bring less hardy plants such as variegated sage or bay under cover, or move them to a sheltered place when frost threatens. Less hardy perennials will often recover from superficial frost, but only if their roots are kept free of frost, so wrap permanent containers in a jacket of sacking or bubble wrap from late autumn until early spring, and cover or mulch the surface to insulate the rootball fully.

Pests and diseases Large-scale commercial growers use regular applications of insecticides and fungicides to produce unblemished crops for sale in supermarkets, and we have been conditioned to expect perfection when buying fresh food. However, if you are more concerned with taste than cosmetic appearance, then these drastic and environmentally harmful measures are unnecessary.

Pests and diseases will occur in all gardens, and you cannot expect to avoid or prevent them completely. It is far more realistic to aim for a low and acceptable level of incidence by creating a healthy garden and maintaining the fertility of the soil. Vigorous plants grown without check in well-tended soil experience less stress and are therefore not as susceptible to problems as are neglected or overcrowded plants in poorly drained, infertile or dry soils. Tender loving care can help to avoid a lot of problems so follow the guidelines given above and in the individual entries.

There is a widening selection of fruit and vegetable varieties resistant to certain pests or diseases, and these are worth trying for their eating qualities. Simple precautions also reduce risks. Mixing and dispersing crops throughout the garden often hides them from pests, while physical barriers such as cloches, fleece, fine-mesh net or a ring of crushed eggshells to deter slugs can protect plants and reduce problems to acceptable proportions. Removing a weak or diseased specimen will often prevent further spread of infection.

Good hygiene is important too, and clearing waste materials removes hiding and breeding sites for pests and diseases. Inspect your crops regularly for early symptoms and act promptly: crushing clusters of yellow eggs under brassica leaves will prevent an invasion of caterpillars, while early aphid arrivals can be knocked off plants with a spray of water. As well as competing for space, light and nutrients, many weeds are related to food plants and share their problems. Control weeds by hoeing, mulching and hand weeding.

Not everything that moves is hostile, and many predator allies such as ladybird feed on familiar pests; similarly, apparent disease symptoms may be harmless physiological disorders. In these cases, treatment sprays may do more harm than good. If problems do reach epidemic proportions, however, you will need to use a fungicide or insecticide, and you should keep one type of each in reserve. Choose the least toxic kind, use no more than is recommended, and apply only on a still evening when pollinating insects are less active.

SOURCES

Below is a selection of specialist suppliers who stock unusual, old or rare varieties of edible plants. Most produce catalogues and offer a mail order service. Also listed are some organizations, books and other information sources that will enable you to find out more about kitchen gardening.

SEEDS

J W Boyce
Bush Pasture
Fordham
Ely, Cambs CB7 5JU
(01638) 721158

D T Brown & Co Ltd
Station Road
Poulton-le-Fylde
Lancs FY6 7HX
(0800) 731 1231

Ferme de Sainte Marthe
PO Box 358
Walton
Surrey KT12 4YX
(01932) 266630

Future Foods
PO Box 1564
Wedmore
Somerset BS28 4DP

S E Marshall & Co Ltd
Wisbech
Cambs PE13 2RF
(01945) 583407

Mr Fothergill's Seeds
Kentford, Newmarket
Suffolk CB8 7QB
(01638) 552512

The Organic Garden Catalogue
Riverdene Business Park
Molesey Road
Hersham
Surrey KT12 4RG
(01932) 253666

W Robinson & Sons Ltd
Sunny Bank
Forton, nr Preston
Lancs PR3 0BN
(01524) 791210

HERB PLANTS

Jekka's Herb Farm
Rose Cottage
Shellard's Lane
Bristol
Avon BS12 2SY
(01454) 418878

Poyntzfield Herb Nursery
Balblair
Black Isle
by Dingwall
Ross & Cromarty
Scotland IV7 8LX
(01381) 610352

Salley Gardens
Flat 3
3 Millicent Road
Nottingham NG2 7LD
(01602) 821366.

Suffolk Herbs
Monks Farm
Coggeshall Road
Kelvedon
Essex CO5 9PG
(01376) 572456

FRUIT PLANTS

Keepers Nursery
Gallants Court
Gallants Lane
East Farleigh

Maidstone
Kent ME15 0LE
(01622) 726465

Reads Nursery
Hales Hall
Loddon
Norfolk NR14 6NS
(01508) 548395

ORGANIZATIONS

Brogdale Horticultural Trust
Brogdale Rd
Faversham
Kent ME13 8XZ
(01795) 535286

Henry Doubleday Research Association
Ryton Organic Gardens
Coventry
West Midlands CV8 3LG
(01203) 303517

Permaculture Association
PO Box 1
Buckfastleigh
Devon TQ11 0LH

Royal Horticultural Society
PO Box 313
80 Vincent Square
London SW1P 2PE
(0171-834) 4333

The Tomato Growers Club
27 Meadowbrook
Old Oxted
Surrey RH8 9LT

BOOKS

The Art of French Vegetable Gardening, Louisa Jones, Artisan 1995

Growing Fruit Trees, Bonham Bazeley, Collins 1990

Herb & Kitchen Garden Design, Andi Clevely; Letts 1993

The Kitchen Garden, Andi Clevely, Conran Octopus 1995

The Kitchen Garden Month-by-Month, Andi Clevely, David & Charles 1998

Jekka's Complete Herb Book, Jekka McVicar, Kyle Cathie 1997

Plants for a Future, Ken Fern, Permanent Publications 1997

Rare Vegetables for Garden and Table, J Organ, Faber 1960

Vegetables from Small Gardens, Joy Larkcom, Faber 1986 New edition

MAGAZINES

Although most gardening magazines include a few articles about growing food crops, *The Kitchen Garden* is a specialist UK monthly packed with stimulating information to whet every gardener's appetite. *The Kitchen Gardener* is an American periodical with a fascinating web site: http://www.taunton.com/kg.

WEBSITES

There is a huge and growing community of gardening sites on the Internet, including forums for sharing problems and information with like-minded gardeners. Simply type 'gardening' in any search engine, or start browsing the sites listed on: http://www.gardenweb.com/vl (or its smaller British address http://www.uk.gardenweb.com).

INDEX

Page numbers in *italics* indicate illustrations.

ACKNOWLEDGMENTS

The publisher would like to thank the following photographers and organizations for their kind permission to reproduce the photographs in this book:

9 Andrew Lawson (Designer: Anne Maynard); 11 left Howard Rice; 11 right Howard Rice (Designer: Toby Buckland);12 Juliette Wade/The Garden Picture Library;14 Andrew Lawson (Old Rectory Cottage, Sudborough, Northants); 15 Sunniva Harte (Old Rectory Cottage, E.Sussex); 16 Courtesy of *The Kitchen Gardener* Magazine; 19 Harpur Garden Library (Designer: Val Gerry); 20 Andrew Lawson (Rofford Manor, Oxon); 22 Maggie Oster (Cedar Falls); 23 Mise au Point; 24 Courtesy of *The Kitchen Gardener* magazine; 27 Mise au Point; 28 Roger Foley (Longwood Gardens); 29 Andrew Lawson; 30 Harpur Garden Library (Designer: Rick Mather); 33 Sunniva Harte/The Garden Picture Library; 34 Harpur Garden Library; 35 John Glover/The Garden Picture Library; 40 Deidi von Schaewen; 46 Christi Carter/The Garden Picture Library; 49 Hugh Palmer; 53 John Glover/The Garden Picture Library; 63 John Glover

The following photographs were specially taken for Conran Octopus:
Nicola Browne 41, 50, 66, 69, 70, 75, 76, 81, 83, 84, 86, 87, 89, 90, 94, 96, 102, 103, 107, 108, 110, 112, 133, 135
Georgia Glynn-Smith 5, 7, 8, 17, 26, 42, 44–45, 54, 56, 59, 60, 62, 64, 73, 74, 78, 93, 98, 101, 104, 109, 115, 116–117, 118, 120, 122, 124–125, 127, 129, 130, 134

The publisher would like to thank the following for providing props for the special photography: Bluebird, Clifton Nurseries, the Conran Shop and Oggetti. They would also like to thank Max Waldren.